Scruffy, but sought-af

D1144779

LEARN TO PLAY GUITAR

Louisa Somerville and Tim Pells
Edited by Cheryl Evans and Jenny Tyler
Designed by Chris Scollen

Contents

Illustrated by: Kuo Kang Chen,
Steve Cross, Brenda Haw, John Beswick, Guy Smith and Teri Gower.
Hand lettering by John McPherson.
With thanks to Terry Munday and Robbie Gladwell.

About learning to play the guitar

Once you know a few basic guitar skills, you can play a great variety of tunes. This book will show you how to start to play, even if you have never picked up a guitar before and no matter what type of guitar you have.

When you first try a new technique it may seem quite difficult. You will need plenty of practice and it is worth mastering one technique thoroughly before moving on to the next. If something sounds odd when you first try it, keep practising slowly until it sounds right. Build up speed as you become more confident and your fingers get stronger and nimbler. Once familiar with the basics, you will find it easier to progress to the more advanced stages.

Types of guitar

You can learn to play nearly all styles of music on almost any guitar. However, some types of guitar are more suited to a particular style, as described here. For information on choosing a guitar and price ranges, turn to the buyer's guide on page 58.

Acoustic guitars

You produce sounds from an acoustic guitar by striking the strings and making them vibrate. The guitar is made of wood with a hollow body to amplify the sound of the vibrating strings. You can use an acoustic for any style except where you need a very loud sound such as in heavy metal music.

Machine heads fixed to each side of the head.

Head

Nut

Neck

Fingerboard

Nylon strings

The machine heads on steel-string guitars are fixed at the back of the head.

Great names:
(Nylon acoustic) – Ramirez 1-A,
Dieter Hopf La Portentosa.

Body

Sound hole

The saddle holds the strings at the correct height.

Soundboard

The bridge passes vibrations from the strings to the soundboard.

Markers inlaid into the fingerboard help you find finger positions.

Steel strings are wound with silver, nickel or bronze.

Nylon-string acoustic guitars

Nylon-string guitars give a full, ▲ round sound suitable for most styles. They are a good choice for a beginner, because the strings are easy to press down. They are also the cheapest sort of guitar to buy. Classical and flamenco guitarists always use nylon-string acoustics.

Steel-string acoustic guitars

◀ Steel-string guitars are often slightly larger than nylon- string guitars and they have a less rounded shape. Steel-string guitars are commonly used in folk and blues music (see pages 10 and 16). They can also be used in jazz and rock music. They make a harder, tinnier sound than a nylon-string guitar.

A plastic fingerplate protects the soundboard on steel-string guitars.

Great names:
(Steel-string acoustic) – Martin D45,
Gibson J200.

2

Electric guitars

An electric guitar has steel strings and a solid body. The body can be various shapes and is usually made of wood; but other materials such as fibreglass are sometimes used. It produces sound when it is plugged into an amplifier and loudspeaker. Electric guitars are more commonly used in stage performances than acoustics because they can make more noise. They are ideal for rock, heavy metal and funky music.

Great names:
(Electric) – Fender Stratocaster, Gibson Les Paul

Steel strings

Fret markers

Pick-ups (see right).

Coil tap (see right).

In/out phase selector switch (see right).

Tone and volume controls.

Guitar lead plugs into output socket and is connected to an amplifier.

Great names:
(Hollow body) – Gibson Super 400
(Semi-acoustic) – Gibson ES-335

F-shaped soundhole

Pick-ups

Longer neck

Four strings

Great names:
(Bass) – Fender Precision, Warwick Bass.

Bass guitars

Electric basses have special strings, make lower sounds than other kinds of guitar and are used to provide bass accompaniment to other instruments. You usually play individual notes on them instead of chords. Four string bass guitars have become very popular in recent years and are now indispensable in most bands. If you want to play bass, turn to page 32 for more information.

Pick-ups

Pick-ups are magnets which convert the vibrations from the strings into electric signals. There are two sorts: single coil pick-ups give a clear sound and double coil (humbucking) give a fuller sound.

A guitar fitted with a double coil pick-up, a coil tap and an in/out of phase switch is the most versatile. The coil tap enables you to change to single coil when you want a crisper sound. An in/out phase allows you to switch between a clean sound (in phase), and a hollow sound (out of phase).

Double coil pick-up

Hollow body guitars and semi-acoustic guitars

Hollow body guitars (sometimes called f-hole or cello guitars) are not so common. They have enough acoustic sound for practising but otherwise need an amplifier. Semi-acoustic guitars are similar with a narrower body.

Styles of playing

This book introduces the basic skills of different musical styles such as rock, reggae, heavy metal and folk. Many such styles have common roots so that once you have learnt the techniques, you can use them to play a wide variety of music, according to your interests.

There are tunes for you to practise. Some of the tunes have two parts. You can play these with a friend, or, if you prefer, play both parts yourself by recording one of them first. There are recording tips on page 40.

Don't worry if you can't read music. All the terms and symbols used in the tunes are explained in the book. There is a glossary of technical terms on page 60.

Getting started

As you learn to play a guitar, you must find a way to hold it comfortably. You can stand or sit, supporting the guitar with an adjustable strap.

Hold the guitar quite high so you can move both arms easily. Your left hand must be free to move along the neck of the guitar while your right hand plucks single strings or strums across them all.

To play classical guitar style (see pages 26-27), sit as shown below.

Start off by holding an electric, acoustic or ▶ electric bass guitar like this. As you get more used to playing you can gradually adjust your position.

Left-handed players

Even if you are left-handed, it is best to hold the guitar as a right-handed player does. If this feels awkward, you can restring an electric guitar in reverse order, then hold the guitar neck in your right hand. Do not restring an acoustic guitar as this can cause tuning difficulties.

Keep the neck higher than the body of the guitar.

Bend your hand round as much as possible.

Neck

Relax your arm and wrist. You don't need to grip the guitar too tightly.

Body

Try to keep your back straight.

Press down firmly with your fingertips.

▲ The picture above shows a close-up of the left-hand position. Put your left thumb behind the neck and curve your fingers to press down on the strings with the tips. Guitarists tend to keep their left fingernails short to make pressing easier.

Right hand plucks the strings just behind the soundhole (to the left of it, as you look at this picture).

Support the guitar so your arms can move freely.

Soundhole

Use a footstool or a pile of books to raise your knee so you do not hunch over the guitar.

Sit forward on the chair.

Classical guitar style

◀ There is one correct way of holding a nylon-string acoustic guitar to play classical style. You sit, supporting it on your left thigh. This leaves your right hand free to pluck the strings to get a good sound. You may need to raise your left thigh, as shown below.

Or use a cushion to raise the guitar on your thigh.

Performance styles

Many pop guitarists develop a way of holding their instruments to suit their own playing style. Level 42's Mark King, shown here, holds his bass guitar high so he can curve his right hand below the strings and hit them with his thumb, making a "slapping" sound.

Mark King

Pete Townshend of The Who used a low-slung guitar to strike power chords (see pages 18-19), with his famous "windmill" arm action.

Tuning up

Before starting to play you need to make sure the strings are in tune with each other. The easiest way to do this is by the fifth fret trick, described at the bottom of the page. The picture below shows the parts of a guitar and other information you should know about before you tune it.

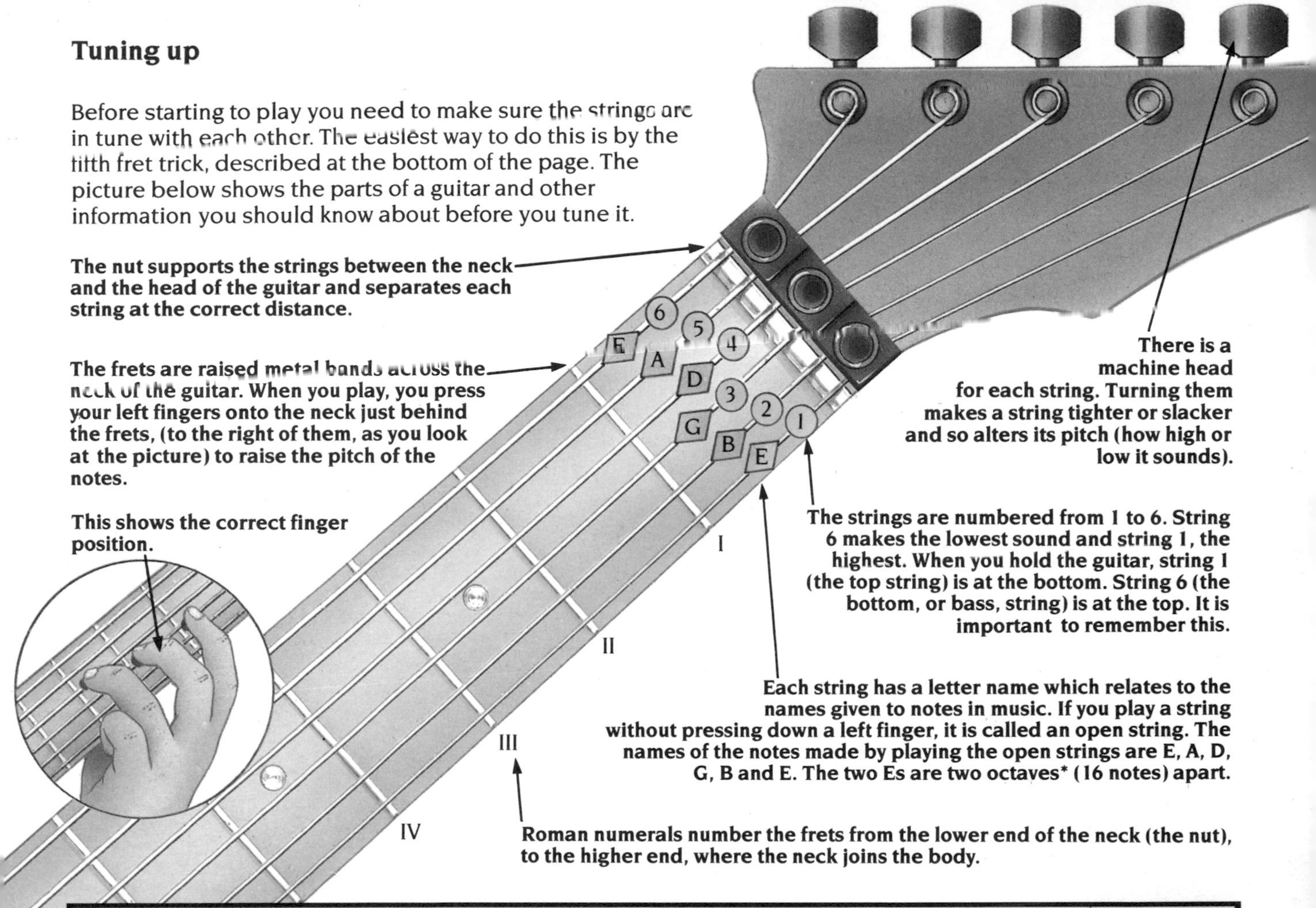

The nut supports the strings between the neck and the head of the guitar and separates each string at the correct distance.

The frets are raised metal bands across the neck of the guitar. When you play, you press your left fingers onto the neck just behind the frets, (to the right of them, as you look at the picture) to raise the pitch of the notes.

This shows the correct finger position.

There is a machine head for each string. Turning them makes a string tighter or slacker and so alters its pitch (how high or low it sounds).

6 5 4
E A D 3
G 2 1
B E

I

II

III

IV

The strings are numbered from 1 to 6. String 6 makes the lowest sound and string 1, the highest. When you hold the guitar, string 1 (the top string) is at the bottom. String 6 (the bottom, or bass, string) is at the top. It is important to remember this.

Each string has a letter name which relates to the names given to notes in music. If you play a string without pressing down a left finger, it is called an open string. The names of the notes made by playing the open strings are E, A, D, G, B and E. The two Es are two octaves* (16 notes) apart.

Roman numerals number the frets from the lower end of the neck (the nut), to the higher end, where the neck joins the body.

The fifth fret trick

This method of tuning is known as the fifth fret trick because you use the fifth fret to check that the strings are in tune. You can see how to do this below. (Before you start, make sure string 6 is pitched correctly, see below right.)

1 With any finger, press down on string 6 just behind the fifth fret. Pluck string 6, then pluck open string 5. If they sound the same, they are in tune with each other.

Turn machine head to adjust the pitch. ↓

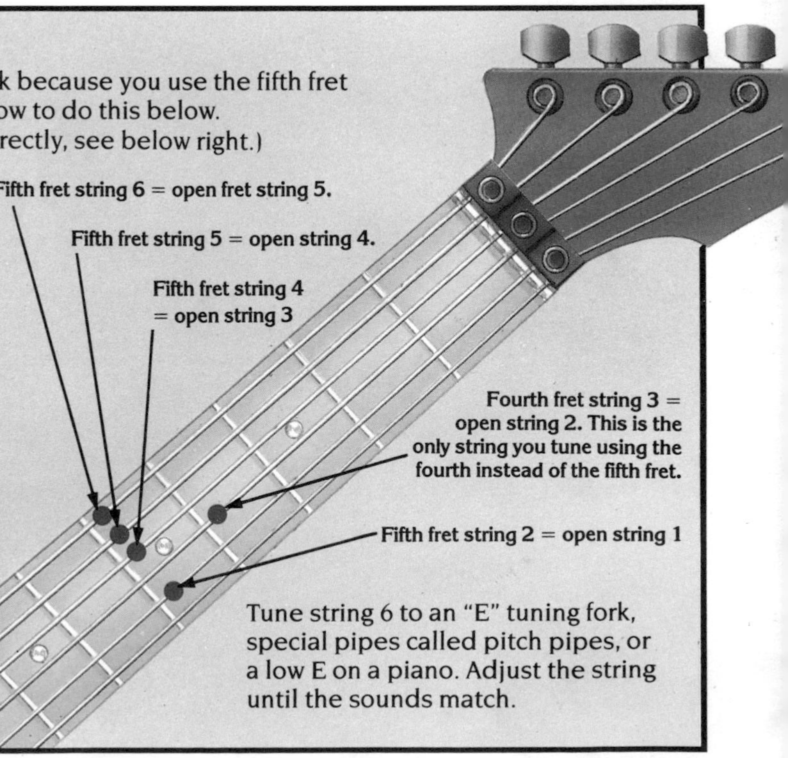

2 If they sound different, ▶ keep plucking both strings and turn the machine head of open string 5 until the sounds match.

3 Keep matching the sound of each string to the one below it, as shown on the right.

Fifth fret string 6 = open fret string 5.

Fifth fret string 5 = open string 4.

Fifth fret string 4 = open string 3

Fourth fret string 3 = open string 2. This is the only string you tune using the fourth instead of the fifth fret.

Fifth fret string 2 = open string 1

Tune string 6 to an "E" tuning fork, special pipes called pitch pipes, or a low E on a piano. Adjust the string until the sounds match.

---

* You can find out more about octaves on page 12.

Playing chords

A simple way to use a guitar to accompany yourself singing is by strumming chords (groups of notes). Most chords are made up of notes that sound good together. Some, though, consist of notes that deliberately jar.

You play chords by pressing some of the strings down on to the guitar neck with your left hand and strumming across all the strings or plucking individual ones with your right hand.

Reading a chord diagram

Chords that are played on the first four frets are shown on diagrams like the one on the right. Each vertical line represents a string on the guitar. The numbers at the top of the diagram tell you which left finger goes on which string.

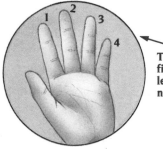

This is how the fingers on your left hand are numbered.

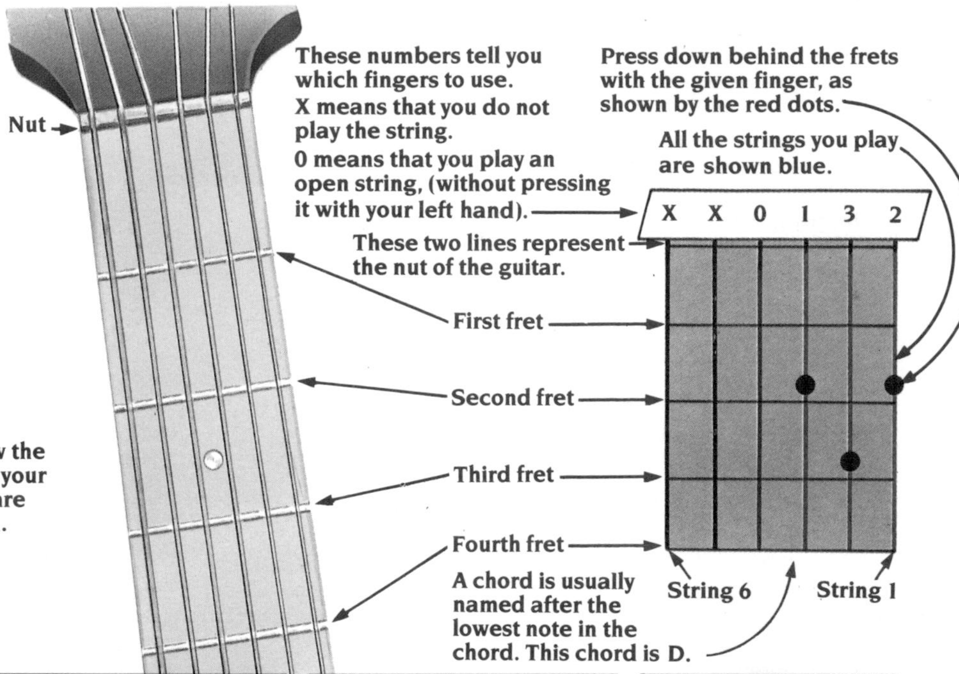

These numbers tell you which fingers to use. X means that you do not play the string. 0 means that you play an open string, (without pressing it with your left hand).

These two lines represent the nut of the guitar.

Press down behind the frets with the given finger, as shown by the red dots.

All the strings you play are shown blue.

Nut

First fret

Second fret

Third fret

Fourth fret

X	X	0	1	3	2

String 6   String 1

A chord is usually named after the lowest note in the chord. This chord is D.

Strumming the chord of D

Try strumming the chord of D, following the step-by-step instructions on the right. If it does not make a clear, musical sound when you first strum it, check that each left finger is pressing hard on one string only.

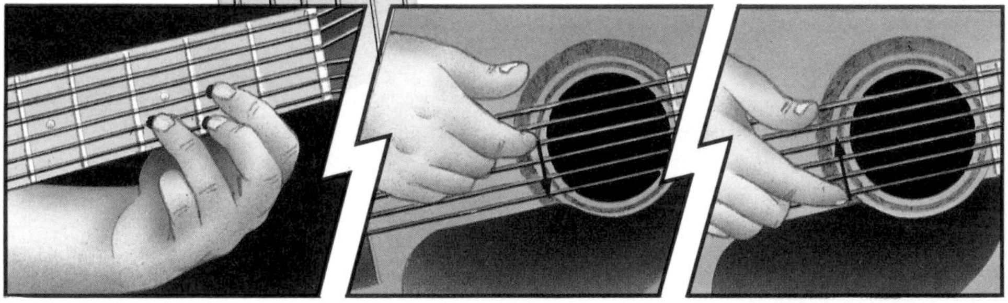

"Finger" the chord by putting your left-hand fingers in position as shown on the chord diagram above.

Sweep the strings firmly downwards with your right first fingernail, avoiding strings 5 and 6. This is called a downstroke.

You can use upstrokes as well. Try strumming down and up alternately and regularly to make a rhythm.

The bass/chord strum

You can make a strum more interesting by plucking the bass (lowest) note of the chord before strumming down the rest of the strings, as shown here using the E chord. This is called a bass/chord strum.

Finger the E chord (see chord chart, right) with your left hand. Pluck the bass note (string 6) with the side of your right thumb. Then strum the other strings with the back of your right first fingernail.

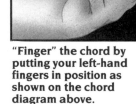

0	2	3	1	0	0

E

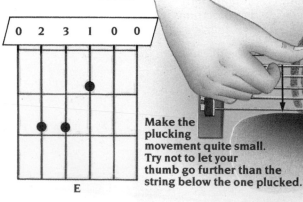

Make the plucking movement quite small. Try not to let your thumb go further than the string below the one plucked.

Finger picking

Finger picking is a style you often hear in folk music. Each string is plucked separately, rather than strummed. Try the finger picking exercise on the right. Repeat it until you can play it smoothly, making an even, rippling sound.

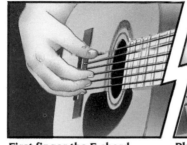

First finger the E chord with your left hand, then rest your right thumb and first, second and third fingers on strings 6,3,2 and 1, respectively.

Pluck string 6 down with your right thumb. Then pluck the other strings up in turn with your right fingertips. Try to keep the rhythm regular.

For a change, pluck string 5 or 4 with your thumb and play strings 3,2 and 1 in another order. Always pluck the same string with the same finger.

Using a plectrum

A plectrum, or pick, can be used instead of your fingernails to pluck guitar strings. It is usually a small, flat, roughly triangular piece of plastic. On an electric or steel-string acoustic guitar, a plectrum gives a louder, fuller tone. Classical guitarists never play with a plectrum. They always use their fingernails.

Plectrums can be bought in light, medium or heavy weights; a light one gives a thin, clear tone; a heavy one gives a solid, round sound; a medium one will give you something in between. Start with a medium or light one, as these are easiest to use. ▶

You hold a plectrum between the thumb and first finger of your right hand. To practise using it, hold down the E chord shown on the previous page, then pick each string separately with the plectrum, starting with string 6. Then try a smooth strum of all the strings. ▶

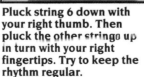

You strike the string with the tip of the plectrum.

Coping with sore fingers

Your left fingertips may get sore when you first start playing chords, but they should toughen up with practice. If they still hurt, check that the "action" (the distance you have to press the strings onto the neck of the guitar) is low. If the action is high, try changing to lighter-gauge strings.*

Make sure the tip shows below your thumb.

Try to pluck each string with the same force.

Move your wrist in a curve so the plectrum strikes each string at right angles.

Did you know?

Many different materials have been used as plectrums. About 300 years ago, musicians first began to pluck guitar strings using a goose quill. In the early twentieth century jazz guitarists used pieces of tortoiseshell which were thick and heavy, suitable for playing jazz rhythms. Nowadays, plastic plectrums are often sold in imitation tortoiseshell.

Practice tip

Starting with string 6, pick each ▶ string four times, alternating down and upstrokes. This helps develop your plectrum control. As you get better at it, gradually increase the speed at which you pick the strings.

Find out how to restring a guitar on pages 46-47.

The three chord trick

Learning just three chords will enable you to accompany yourself singing a surprising number of well-known songs. This is known as the three chord trick. There are a number of different sets of three chords which you can use.* The chords in each set always sound good together, as you can see when you try out the ones on these two pages.

Three chord set in A major

Try strumming the three chords shown on the right. Finish the sequence by playing the A chord again at the end. This is known as the key chord. The whole sequence is said to be in the key of A major. Each time you play a chord sequence, begin and end on the key chord.

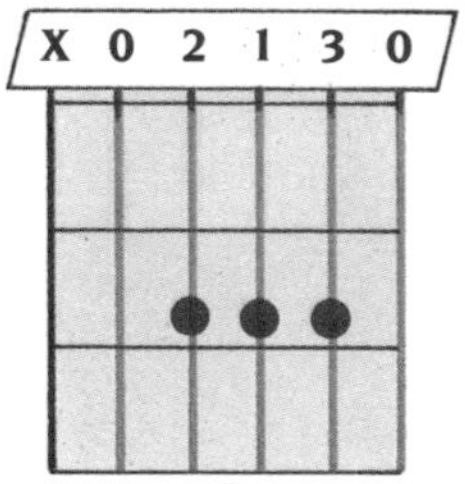

X 0 2 1 3 0

A

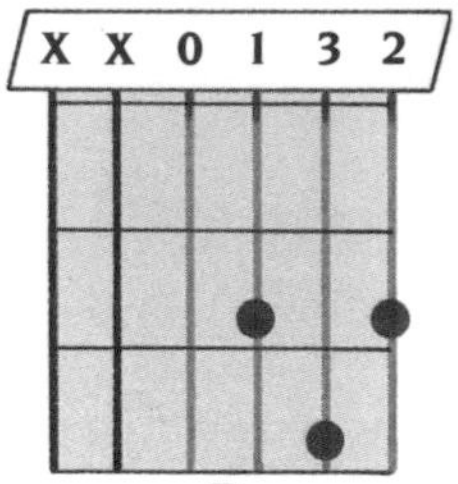

X X 0 1 3 2

D

0 2 0 1 0 0

E7

A chord set in a minor key

Play this chord sequence and compare its sound to the other three-chord sets on this page. It sounds different because it is in what is called a "minor" key. Tunes in a minor key sometimes seem to have a sad quality. This chord set is in the key of A minor.

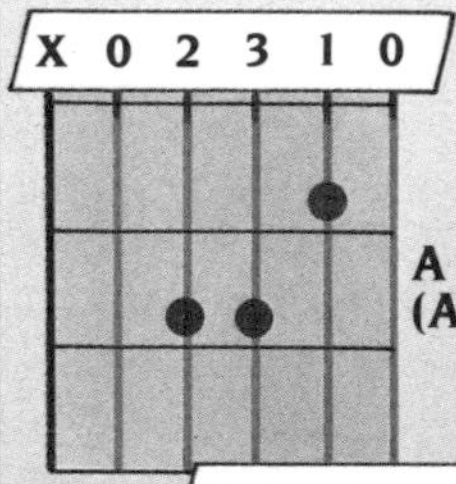

X 0 2 3 1 0

A minor (Am)

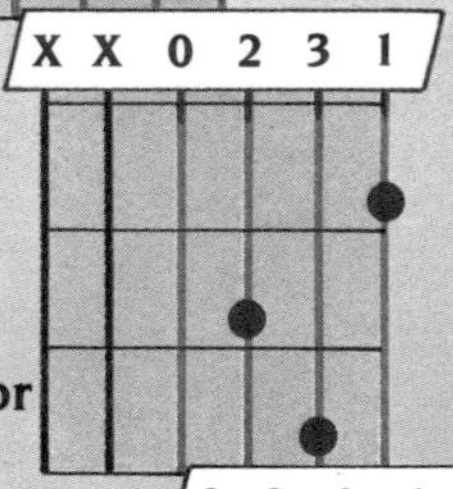

X X 0 2 3 1

D minor (Dm)

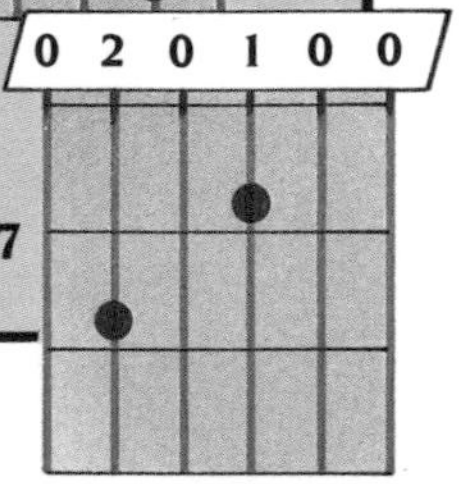

0 2 0 1 0 0

E7

Practise the chords until you can change smoothly from one to another. If you know the song on the right, you can use the chords to accompany yourself singing it, changing chords where marked. If you don't know it, you will find the tune on page 48. (Reading guitar music is explained later in the book.)

FRANKIE AND JOHNNY

A
Frankie and Johnny were lovers,

Oh lordy, how they could love,

D
They swore to be true to each other,

A
True as the stars above,

E7
He was her man,

A
But he done her wrong.

Frankie and Johnny is a traditional American folk ballad. You can hear it on the album "Oh So Good And Blue" by Taj Mahal.

Three chord set in E major

These chords are in the key of E major. You can just as well sing Frankie and Johnny to this three chord set, depending on if you like singing high (A major) or low (E major). Play it as before, only use E instead of A, A instead of D and B7 instead of E7.

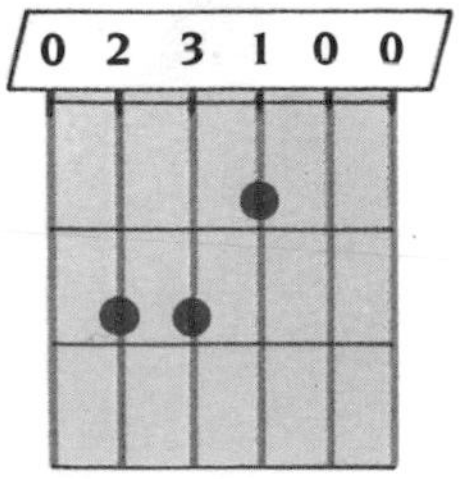

0 2 3 1 0 0

E

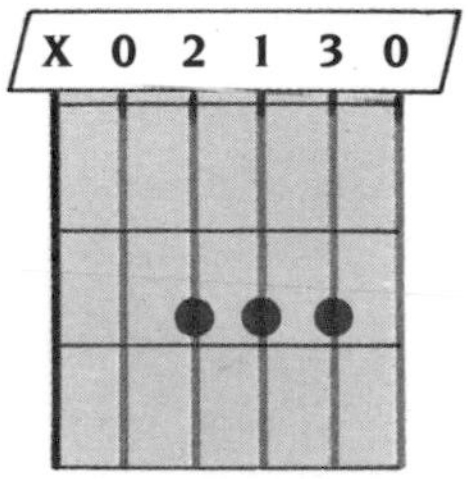

X 0 2 1 3 0

A

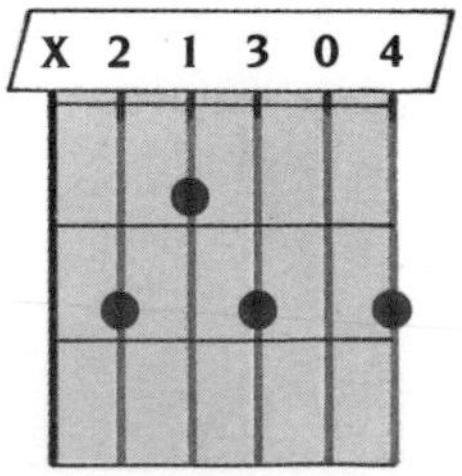

X 2 1 3 0 4

B7

Chord names in three-chord sets

Each chord has a name identifying its place in a set. In the A major set the names of the chords are as shown on the right.

A	Tonic

The tonic, or key chord, usually begins and ends a tune.

D	Sub-dominant

The sub-dominant chord is the second chord in a three-chord set.

E7	Dominant 7th

The dominant 7th chord is the third chord and leads back to the tonic.

Three chord set in C

Use this chord set in the key of C to play the Country Strum in the box. This is another tune with a typical American folk music feel. You could use the bass/chord strum (see page 6) to liven it up.

This sign shows where you cover more than one string with one finger.

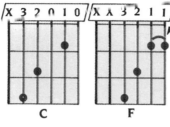

X 3 2 0 1 0   X X 3 2 1 1

C   F

Country Strum

C	F	C	F
C	F	G7	C

Strum each chord four times before changing to the next one.

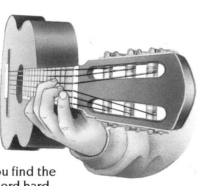

3 2 0 0 0 1

G7

If you find the F chord hard to play, leave the first string open. This gives the chord F major 7, which harmonizes with the rest of the set in C major. You can use F major 7 instead of F major until your hand is agile enough to cover two strings with one finger.

First finger covers strings 1 and 2 when playing the F chord.

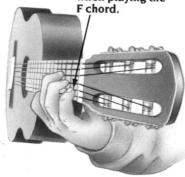

Technique tip

It helps quick chord changes if you can keep some fingers on the strings between chords. For example, first play the A chord.

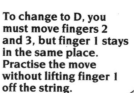

To change to D, you must move fingers 2 and 3, but finger 1 stays in the same place. Practise the move without lifting finger 1 off the string.

For E7, lift up fingers 2 and 3, slide finger 1 down one fret along the string, then replace finger 2 in the correct position. Look out for ways to apply this tip to other chord changes.

Taking time to practise

It is worth spending some time practising these three chord sets, as the quicker and smoother your chord changes, the better your playing will sound (even if you only know three chords). It is a good idea to concentrate on one set until you are really happy with it before moving on to another one.

You need to be confident of chord changing before you tackle different styles and techniques later on.

Playing the blues

A lot of modern music is based on a style called the blues. Blues music uses chord sequences based on the three-chord trick, with a distinctive rhythm, called the blues or boogie rhythm. Bands such as ZZ Top use this rhythm to create a blues-based sound.

The boogie rhythm

You can practise this rhythm on any chord, so finger one you know. The rhythm has four counts, each divided into three beats (see right). To play the rhythm, say, "One, two, three," four times, slowly and evenly. Strum down each time you say "one" and "three". Don't strum on "two". Then try counting and playing faster.

What is the 12-bar blues?

A bar is a group of counts. For example, the boogie rhythm above is a bar of four counts. Most blues music is played in a pattern of 12 bars, often called the 12-bar blues.

The first sequence on the right is a 12-bar blues tune, using the three-chord set in A (see previous page). Play it using the boogie rhythm so each bar has four counts. Finger the A chord and play eight downstrokes in the boogie rhythm. Repeat three times, then play the D chord, and so on.

This second sequence shows you the chord pattern of the 12-bar blues, using the names that identify a chord's position in a three-chord set (tonic, sub-dominant or dominant 7th). Play the 12-bar blues following this pattern, using any three-chord set.*

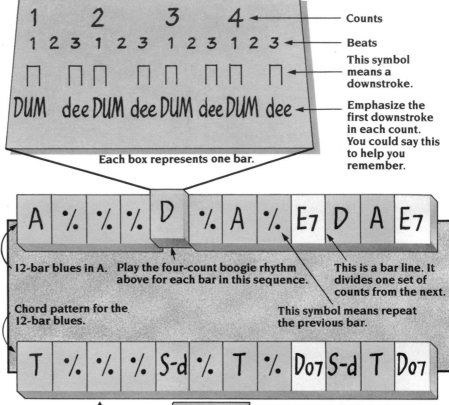

Counts

Beats

This symbol means a downstroke.

Emphasize the first downstroke in each count. You could say this to help you remember.

Each box represents one bar.

12-bar blues in A.

Play the four-count boogie rhythm above for each bar in this sequence.

This is a bar line. It divides one set of counts from the next.

Chord pattern for the 12-bar blues.

This symbol means repeat the previous bar.

Colour code	T	Tonic
	S-d	Sub-dominant
	Do7	Dominant 7th

History of the blues

The blues developed in America in the last century. It was a blend of tribal rhythms, brought from Africa by slaves, and traditional European folk music. Played mostly on banjos and guitars at first, the blues became the black American folk music of the early 20th century.

During the 1940s and 50s, guitarists such as Muddy Waters started using electric guitars to play "electric" blues in the bars of Chicago and other cities. Soon, a wider audience was enjoying the blues as stars such as Elvis Presley and Chuck Berry popularized blues styles.

Eric Clapton

John Mayall's Bluesbreakers, formed in Britain in the 1960s, was the first major non-American blues band. This picture shows one of the band, Eric Clapton. His playing had a strong influence on the band's sound and inspired many blues guitarists.

*For a chart of three-chord sets see page 36.

A 12-bar blues shuffle to play

Before you have a go at the blues shuffle ▶ below, you need to learn the sets of two-string chords on the right. Chords like these are typical of the blues sound. When you play them, be careful only to hit the two strings indicated. There are two tonic and two sub-dominant chords in these sets.

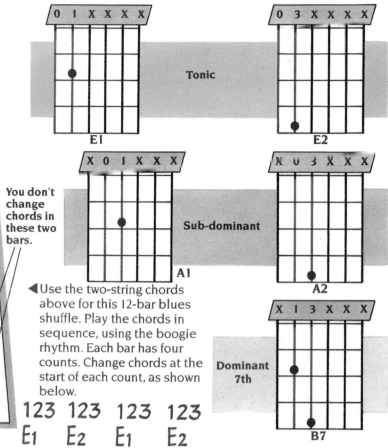

Tonic — E1, E2

Sub-dominant — A1, A2

Dominant 7th — B7

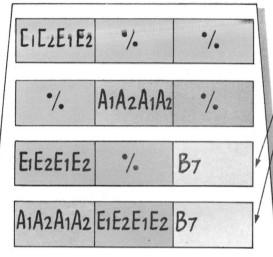

$E_1E_2E_1E_2$	·/·	·/·
·/·	$A_1A_2A_1A_2$	·/·
$E_1E_2E_1E_2$	·/·	B_7
$A_1A_2A_1A_2$	$E_1E_2E_1E_2$	B_7

You don't change chords in these two bars.

◀ Use the two-string chords above for this 12-bar blues shuffle. Play the chords in sequence, using the boogie rhythm. Each bar has four counts. Change chords at the start of each count, as shown below.

123 123 123 123
E_1 E_2 E_1 E_2

Blues shuffle for two

Here is a way for you and a friend to play the 12-bar blues shuffle together. One of you repeats the shuffle, as above. At the same time, the other strums the three-chord sequence in E on the right, using the boogie rhythm.

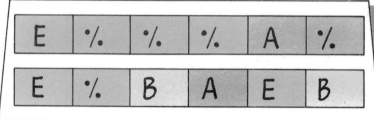

E	·/·	·/·	·/·	A	·/·
E	·/·	B	A	E	B

One of you counts to four before you start, to set the beat.

You can use electric or acoustic guitars.

Try to carry on even if you make a mistake.

Here is a set of two-string ▶ chords in the key of A. Try the blues shuffle using them. The colour code tells you which chord is which in the sequence. A friend could accompany you with the three-chord set in A.

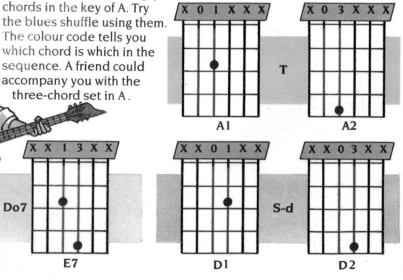

T — A1, A2

Do7 — E7

S-d — D1, D2

11

The blues scale

Once you know the blues scale, you can make up blues tunes and improvise, or invent, solos based on it.* Here you can find out about the blues scale and other musical scales so you can compare them.

Playing the blues scale means playing individual notes. In guitar music, which note to play can be indicated by a method called tablature. Tablature is explained in the box on the left below. You should read this first.

Understanding tablature

Tablature is a way of writing down guitar music. Below you can see how tablature relates to the strings of the guitar and find out how to read it.

String numbers

0 tells you to play an open string.

Six horizontal lines represent the strings of the guitar.

Numbers on the string lines show you which fret to press that string onto while you play it.

Numbers in a vertical line tell you to press the strings in these positions all at the same time and strum a chord.

Read the tablature from left to right. Finger string 6 on the third fret and play it, then play open string 5, and so on.

Finger the frets as you find most comfortable. Most people use their first finger on the first fret, second finger on the second fret, and third and fourth fingers on the third and fourth frets when playing individual notes.

Practise playing the tablature above a few times to get used to the system.

What is a scale?

All notes in music are named after one of the first seven letters of the alphabet. A major music scale is a pattern of eight notes, starting and ending on notes with the same letter name, which sound similar, but one is higher than the other. They are separated by a distance called one octave. Play the major scale shown on the tablature below to hear what it sounds like.

A scale is named after the notes it starts and ends on. This is the scale of C major.

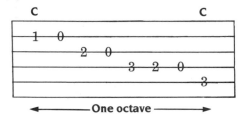

The blues scale

A blues scale starts and ends on notes one octave apart, like the major scale, but has only seven notes altogether, arranged in a different pattern. The tablature below shows the blues scale in G. Play it, then play the major scale in C again to compare them.

Here are the notes of the blues scale in G. The first and last notes are both G.

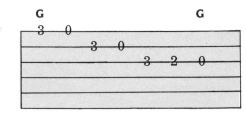

On the next tablature, the blues scale in G has been extended down an octave for you to play.

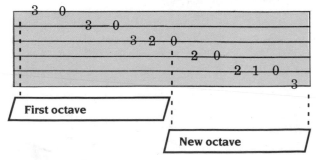

First octave

New octave

*There are ideas for a solo on page 15.

Writing down rhythms

Tablature can also be used to write down the rhythm of a piece of music. The symbols used are related to standard music notation, in which a note of one beat is called a crotchet. A note half as long as a crotchet is called a quaver. These are the standard music symbols for the different notes.

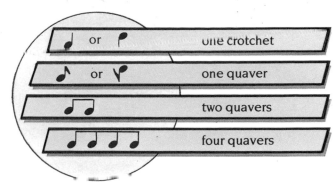

♩ or ♩	one crotchet
♪ or ♪	one quaver
♫	two quavers
♬	four quavers

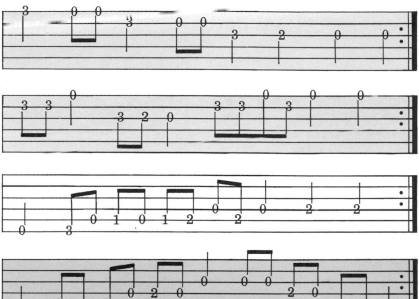

This sign means repeat the whole passage.

The rhythm below is in standard music notation. To play it, count "one and two and three and four and" as shown. As you say each number, pluck once for a crotchet or twice for a pair of quavers. Use any string.

| 1 | + | 2 | + | 3 | + | 4 | + |

When a rhythm is shown on tablature, the head of a crotchet or quaver is replaced by the number of the fret. The four pieces of tablature on the left show musical phrases, called riffs, using notes from the blues scale. Play them, using the rhythms given.

Robert Cray

Flash riffs are still popular with blues players, such as American guitarist Robert Cray.

A classic blues "flash" riff

In the late 1960s, the style of guitarists such as Jimmy Page (with Led Zeppelin) and Eric Clapton (with Cream) became the hallmarks of their bands. If you listen to their albums, you will hear them playing blues scale riffs, like the one below. Practise until you can play it really fast and smoothly to make it "flash".

This beat is divided into three parts. It is called a triplet.

Strum these two notes together.

This is called a tied note. You play one note that lasts for four beats.

Did you know?

Jimmy Page sometimes played his guitar with a violin bow when he played "Whole Lotta Love" live with Led Zeppelin.

Lead guitar

A lead guitarist "leads" the music in a band by playing solo passages, either to introduce a tune or as a riff to replace part of the tune. You make up a solo from single notes by experimenting with what sounds good. You can emphasize the rhythm and mood of a tune or contrast with it, for example.

To play fluent solos, you need to develop your right hand technique. There are skills to learn and ways to practise them below.

String crossing

When you pluck single notes with a plectrum, using both down and upstrokes, you may have to pass over one string without touching it in order to play the next. This is called string crossing and is worth learning to do quickly and accurately. Get the feel of the technique by plucking strings 1 and 2, as shown here, then use it to play the blues scale below.

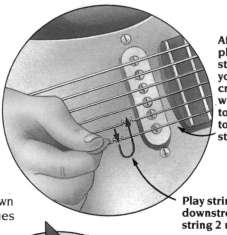

After playing string 1, you must cross back without touching it to play string 2.

Play string 1 downstroke, then string 2 upstroke.

Great guitarists – B.B. King

This picture is of B.B. King, born in Mississippi in 1925. His blend of blues and jazz influenced many 1960s rock guitarists, such as Eric Clapton. B.B. (short for Blues Boy) is known for emotional playing and note-bending.

He is famous for calling all his guitars Lucille after a girl at a concert of his. He saved his guitar from a fire caused by a fight over her.

Improve your string crossing

Use this blues scale in C to improve your string crossing. It is played in fifth position, which means placing your left hand so that finger 1 can press on the strings at the fifth fret, finger 2 at the sixth fret, and so on. You need to get used to playing in fifth position for the tunes on the next page.

Place your hand in fifth position.

Fret the first note with finger 4 on the eighth fret, and so on.

Start with an upstroke, then alternate down and upstrokes.

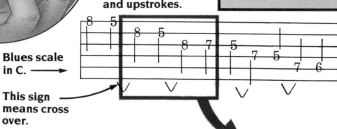

Blues scale in C. →

This sign means cross over.

String bending

You can vary the pitch of a note by bending a string with your left hand as you play it. This makes a moaning sound which lead guitarists use a lot to put feeling into blues music. See how to do it on the right.

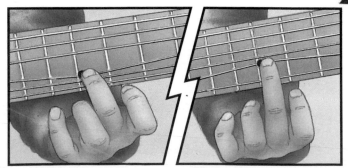

On the lower four strings, pull the string down away from you as you play it.

On strings 1 and 2, push the string up, to avoid pulling it over the edge of the neck.

Now play the blues scale in C again, adding some string bending. The arrows on the part of the scale repeated in this box show especially good notes to bend.

Playing a two-part blues

Here is an interesting way to practise the techniques on the last page. There are two parts, so you can either record one part to accompany yourself or ask a friend to help.

The two chord sequences on the right are one part of the tune. The notes from the blues scale in fifth position, below, are the other.

While one person (or the recording machine) plays the first chord sequence*, the other plays the notes. Then try the second chord sequence to accompany the same notes.

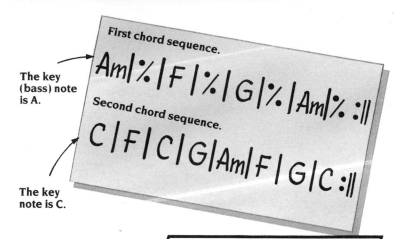

First chord sequence.

The key (bass) note is A.

Am|٪|F|٪|G|٪|Am|٪:||

Second chord sequence.

The key note is C.

C|F|C|G|Am|F|G|C:||

As you play, notice that the effect of playing the same notes with the different chord sequences is surprisingly different. This is because the sequences are in different keys.

This is a tied note. You play one note that lasts for two beats.

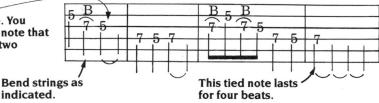

Bend strings as indicated.

This tied note lasts for four beats.

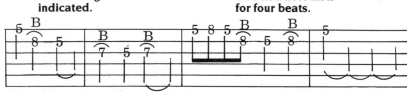

You could try making up your own pattern of notes to play from the blues scale. To be sure it sounds good with these chord sequences, begin and end your pattern on the key note of the sequence you play. (See the blues scale in C, opposite, and in A on page 12.)

Chords in the blues scale

You can use two-string chords from the blues scale in fifth position to improvise good lead solos. The ones shown on the first tablature below sound especially good, so try them out for yourself.

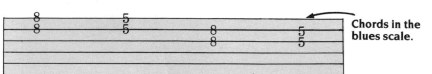

Chords in the blues scale.

On the next tablature, these chords are used for a rock'n'roll solo. Arrows tell you to bend some of the chords. See how to do this in the picture on the right. You could play the solo to introduce the blues shuffle in E on page 11.

Rock'n'roll lead solo.

Great guitarists – Chuck Berry

With his famous "duck walk" and cherry red Gibson guitar, Chuck Berry became a hugely popular performer in the 1950s. Since then, his raunchy blend of country and blues music, known as rock'n'roll, has had a major influence on blues players. He is renowned for his lead solos, like the one at the bottom of this page.

Bend both strings together like this.

Folk music

Folk (or country) music was originally the music of ordinary people. It told the stories of their lives and feelings. Folk guitarists traditionally play solo, accompanying themselves using a plectrum technique called flatpicking, described here. Folk music is usually played on steel-string acoustic guitars, but you can use any kind.

Flatpicking

You can make chords sound folky by playing the bass/chord strum (see page 6), using a plectrum instead of your finger. Try it on the chord of A minor. With a plectrum, pluck the bass note (string 5), then strum down and up the other strings. Combining plucked individual strings and strumming with a plectrum is called flatpicking.

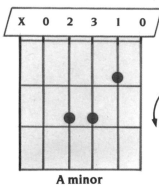

X 0 2 3 1 0

A minor

Think of the rhythm as long, short, short. The long beat is the picked note. The short ones are the strums.

This symbol stands for an upstroke.

The hammer-on technique

Hammering-on is a technique that allows you to sound two consecutive notes from a string, while only plucking it once.

How to do the hammer-on

With a plectrum, pluck open string D (string 4). While the string is still vibrating, press finger 2 down firmly onto it, just behind the second fret. You will hear the note E without having to pluck the string again.

Hammering-on a chord

Here's how to use the same hammer-on while you strum the chord of A minor. Press down fingers 1 and 3, as shown. Pluck string 4 with a plectrum and hammer-onto it with finger 2 on the second fret. Then strum the chord.

This is how you write down a hammer-on. 0 means play an open string. The number after the H tells you which fret to hammer-on.

The story of folk

Bob Dylan

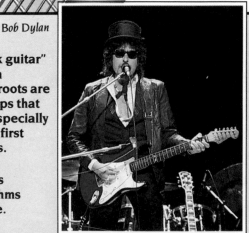

Every part of the world has developed its own style of folk music, drawn from the culture of its people. Because of this, South American folk music is very different to Romanian, say.

Nowadays, the term "folk guitar" is usually associated with American folk music. Its roots are in the many cultural groups that make up America, and especially in the Celtic music of the first Irish and Scottish settlers.

Paul Simon, left, includes many African-based rhythms in his innovative folk style.

One of the most prominent American folk musicians was Woody Guthrie. He sang songs

Paul Simon

about the suffering in the Great Depression of the 1930s. His style influenced singers of the 1960s, such as Bob Dylan.

Flatpicking the Country Blues

The tablature on the right shows the notes and rhythm for a flatpicking chord, using a hammer-on. Follow the pictures and directions below to play it. When you feel happy with the technique, try the Country Blues, beneath, in the same style.

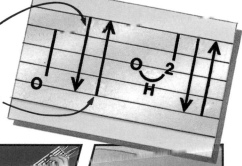

An arrow pointing down means a downstroke.

An arrow like this means an upstroke.

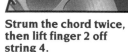

Hold down the A minor chord. Pluck string 5 with the plectrum.

Strum the chord twice, then lift finger 2 off string 4.

Pluck string 4 and hammer-on finger 2.

Strum the chord twice more. Repeat the steps until you perfect them.

Country Blues

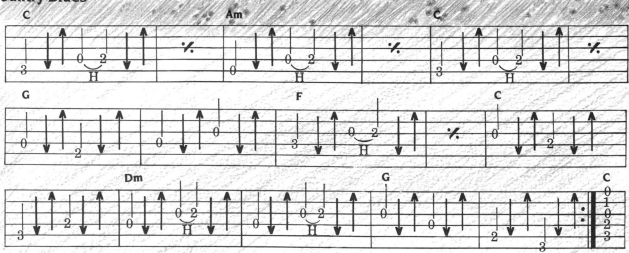

Getting the Hammer-on Blues

On the right are chord diagrams for the three-chord sets in the Hammer-on Blues, below. The black dot shows where you pick an open string, then hammer-on. Play the blues chord sequence, using the rhythm you learnt above.

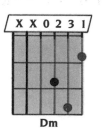
Am — X 0 2 3 1 0

Dm — X X 0 2 3 1

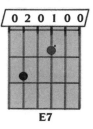
E7 — 0 2 0 1 0 0

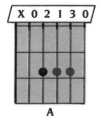
E — 0 2 3 1 0 0

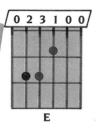
A — X 0 2 1 3 0

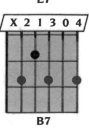
B7 — X 2 1 3 0 4

The Hammer-on Blues

Am| ٪ | ٪ | ٪ |Dm| ٪ |Am|
٪ |E₇|Dm|Am|E₇:|| E₇| ٪ |
٪ | ٪ |Am| ٪ ٪ | E | ٪ |B₇|
Am| E |B₇ ||

17

Heavy metal

Heavy metal is raw, gutsy music which sounds best on electric guitars. It is based on sets of two-string chords, called power chords, and is generally played loud and fast for impact. Power chords are quite easy to play so you can concentrate on the powerful rhythms.

Power chord shape

Most power chords are played with your fingers in the same positions in relation to each other, as shown on the chord diagram and picture below. You can move your fingers in this chord "shape" up and down the neck of the guitar to play power chords on any fret. They sound best on the lower strings.

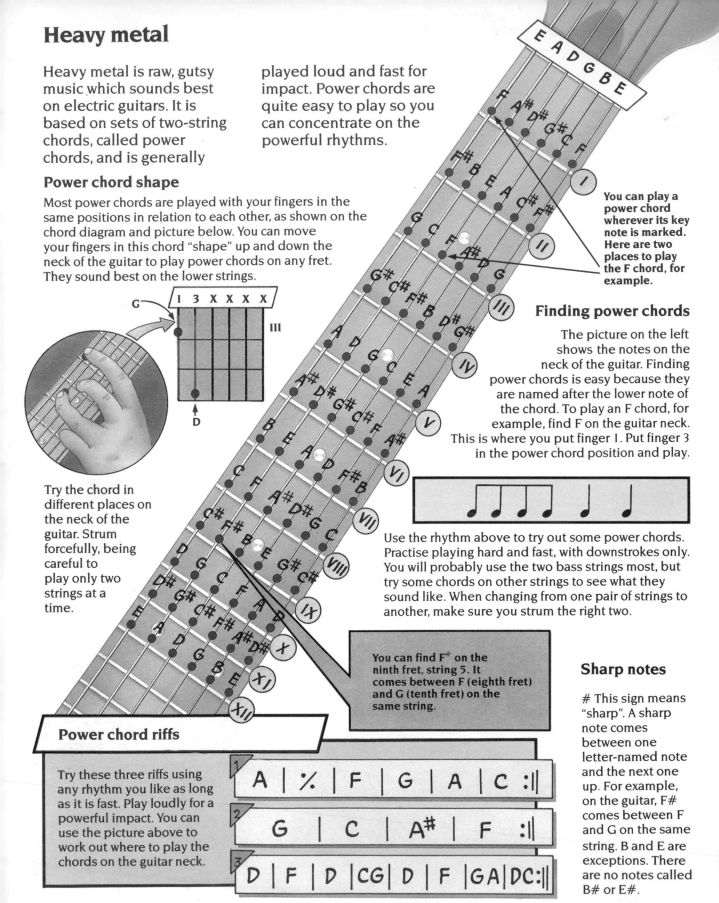

Try the chord in different places on the neck of the guitar. Strum forcefully, being careful to play only two strings at a time.

You can play a power chord wherever its key note is marked. Here are two places to play the F chord, for example.

Finding power chords

The picture on the left shows the notes on the neck of the guitar. Finding power chords is easy because they are named after the lower note of the chord. To play an F chord, for example, find F on the guitar neck. This is where you put finger 1. Put finger 3 in the power chord position and play.

Use the rhythm above to try out some power chords. Practise playing hard and fast, with downstrokes only. You will probably use the two bass strings most, but try some chords on other strings to see what they sound like. When changing from one pair of strings to another, make sure you strum the right two.

You can find F# on the ninth fret, string 5. It comes between F (eighth fret) and G (tenth fret) on the same string.

Sharp notes

This sign means "sharp". A sharp note comes between one letter-named note and the next one up. For example, on the guitar, F# comes between F and G on the same string. B and E are exceptions. There are no notes called B# or E#.

Power chord riffs

Try these three riffs using any rhythm you like as long as it is fast. Play loudly for a powerful impact. You can use the picture above to work out where to play the chords on the guitar neck.

1 A | % | F | G | A | C :||

2 G | C | A# | F :||

3 D | F | D | CG | D | F | GA | DC :||

Pulling-off a note

The pull-off is a technique that can help you to play fast and smoothly by plucking extra notes with your left hand, instead of having to strum them. See how to do it in the pictures on the right.

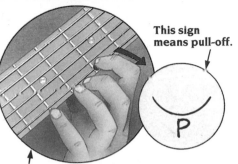

This sign means pull-off.

Press finger 1 behind any fret on string 1 and pluck the string with your other hand. Then pull finger 1 off the string away from you to sound the open string note (E).

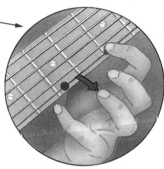

Now try pulling-off to a fretted note. Press finger 1 behind the third fret and finger 3 behind the fifth fret on string 1. Pluck the string and pull off finger 3 to sound the fretted note (G)

Trills

A trill is two notes repeated rapidly. You can play a trill by combining the hammer-on (page 16) and pull-off. This technique is used a lot in heavy metal music. Try playing a trill, as shown on the right. Pluck the string once only.

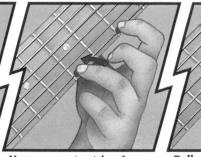

Play string 1 downstroke, pressing with finger 1 on the fifth fret.

Hammer-on to string 1 with finger 3, on the seventh fret.

Pull-off finger 3. Repeat the hammer-on and pull-off several times rapidly.

Using the trill

You can give a power chord sequence a typical heavy metal sound by playing trills over the top. For example, you could record the sequence below, using the heavy metal rhythm on the page opposite. Then play it back while you play the blues riff in C, shown beneath it, playing trills as indicated.

```
 C  | A#  | C  | G# A#  :||
```

Play this note before the first bar.

```
        8 11 8  8              8 11 8  8
 11     H  P   11 8        11  H  P  11 8        10
 B              10 8 10    B              10 8
```

| C | A# | C | G# A# |

You could also try playing trills over the riffs on the page opposite. Use blues scale notes in the same key as each riff.

Technique tip

It will help you to get better results when you play hammer-ons and pull-offs if you can keep the knuckles of your left hand parallel to the neck of the guitar. You could check that your hand position is correct in a mirror.

History of Heavy metal

In the late 1960s, guitarists like Jimi Hendrix and Jeff Beck experimented with creating new, exciting guitar sounds. They emphasized strong bass guitar, loud power chords and overall volume and the resulting sound was called "heavy".

Typical of this aggressive style of playing were Led Zeppelin. On their first album, many tunes were played in a very low key with two bass drums. The effect was loud and powerful.

Heavy metal still has lots of fans. Bands like Motorhead, Def Leppard and Bon Jovi, are playing this kind of music successfully today.

Jon Bon Jovi

Reggae

Reggae music is easily recognized by its distinctive, off-beat rhythms and repetitive beat. You can get the feel of it by trying the rhythms on these two pages, using some typical reggae chords.

The off-beat rhythm

In most music the first and third beats of a four-beat bar are stronger than the second and fourth. In reggae music it is the other way round – the second and fourth beats (called off-beats) are emphasized. To make the reggae sound, you play only on these off-beats, usually using chords in positions high up the neck.

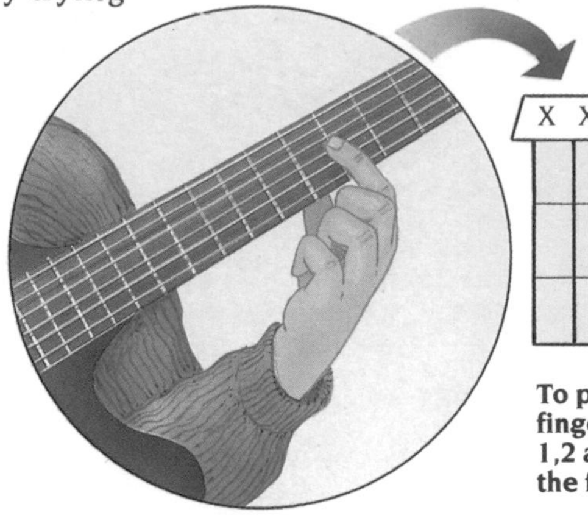

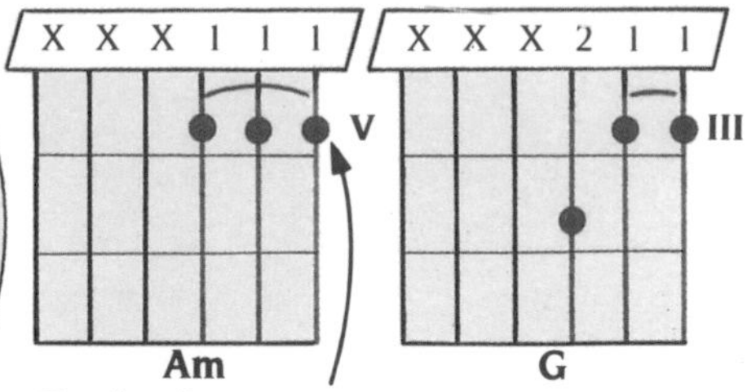

Am

To play Am, press finger 1 on strings 1,2 and 3 behind the fifth fret.

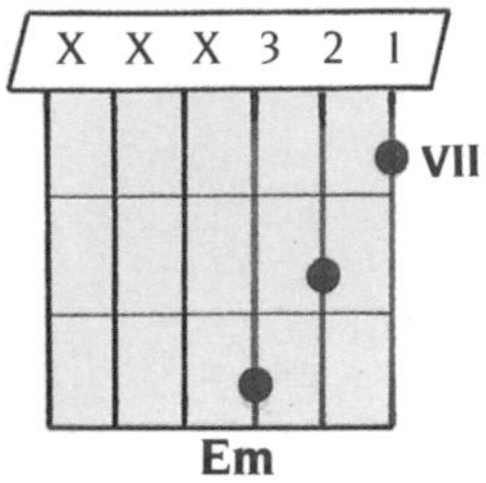

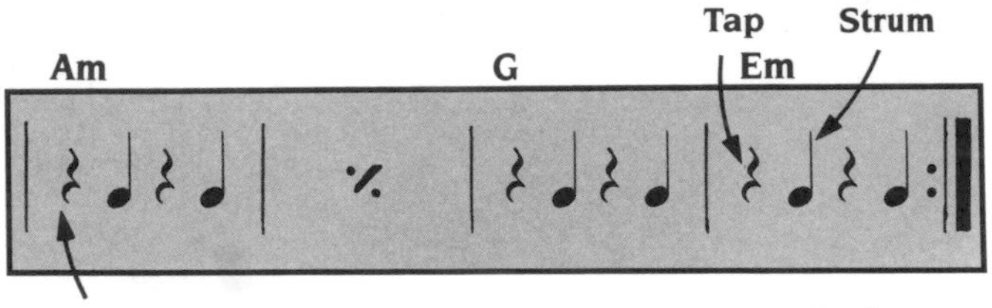

G

Em

Use the chords above to play the off-beat rhythm on the left. The picture shows how you finger the Am chord.

Tap   Strum

Am   **G**   **Em**

This symbol is called a crotchet rest. It is used to show where you do not play for one beat.

You may find it helps to tap your foot on each rest to keep the beat.

The chop

This is a way of playing chords so that they sound short, or cut-off. To do it, you stop the strings vibrating immediately after playing them, as shown below. What you do with your left hand is called damping the strings and is a widely-used technique. The chop gets its name from the chopping action of the right hand.

Strum the chord, then release the pressure in your fingers but keep them lightly on the strings.

To stop the strings vibrating completely, bring your right hand down on the strings as you lift your left hand.

History of reggae

The strong beat of Jamaican reggae music developed from a combination of Spanish dance rhythms and African tribal rhythms brought to Jamaica by slaves.

During the 1960s, big bands played a kind of instrumental music called ska, which combined these traditional rhythms and blues rhythms. Gradually the ska sound changed as the bands became smaller. People started to add words, influenced by Jamaican work songs and the Rastafarian religion. The new style of music became known as reggae. Probably the most famous reggae band was Bob Marley and the Wailers. Their songs had a strong beat and often political lyrics.

Bob Marley

The clave rhythm

This West Indian rhythm is traditionally played on the claves, a pair of hardwood sticks. They are banged together to give a very sharp, piercing sound. The rhythm was first played on the guitar by Bo Diddley, an American rock'n'roll player. Since then it has been adopted by many other guitarists. Have a go at the clave rhythm as shown below, using the Am chord.

| ♩. | ♩. | ♩ | ♩ | | 𝄽 ♩ | ♩ | 𝄽 |
| 1 + | 2 + | 3 + | 4 + | | 1 + 2 + | 3 + | 4 + |

A dot after a note means it lasts half as long again; so this dotted crotchet lasts for one and a half beats.

Reggae tune

Many reggae tunes have their roots in American gospel music. You can give the gospel song below a lively reggae sound by playing it with the clave rhythm or the off-beat rhythm. If you play bass guitar, you can accompany the tune with the reggae bass line on page 33.

The tune is shown in tablature. If you are not familiar with the song, try out the tune and sing along to it. Then play the rhythm and sing the words.

the reggae bass line on page 33.

Did you know?

Bo Diddley had guitars made for him in various unusual shapes such as squares and rectangles. This picture shows one of his favourites.

Am ... **G**

Joshua fit the battle of ‿ Je‿richo ‿, Je‿richo ‿,

Am   ↖ "Fit" means fought.

Je‿richo ‿. Joshua fit the battle of ‿ Je‿richo   and the

Em   **Am**

walls   came   tumbling   down ‿

Flamenco guitar

One of the most dramatic guitar styles is the Spanish folk style called flamenco. It is usually played fast, with a strong rhythm and sounds best on a special flamenco guitar.

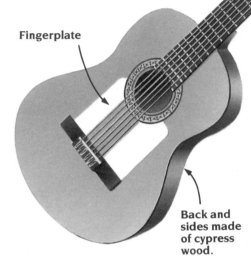

Fingerplate

Back and sides made of cypress wood.

Flamenco guitars are usually a bit smaller than classical ones.

A flamenco guitar is similar to a classical guitar. The back and sides are usually made of cypress wood instead of rosewood or mahogany, which helps the instrument produce more volume.

Flamenco guitarists often strike and tap the guitar as part of the rhythm. A flamenco guitar has special plastic fingerplates to protect the wood.

The story of flamenco

Flamenco is more than just a musical style. The word means "like a gypsy". It describes the culture of the gypsies of Andalusia, in southern Spain.

Typical Andalusian street scene.

Between the 8th and 15th centuries, southern Spain was occupied by an Arab people called Moors. As a result, flamenco music was strongly influenced by Arabic styles.

Flamenco dancers.

Singing and dancing to flamenco music are traditional. The rhythm is accentuated by heel-stamping, hand-clapping and by clicking pieces of curved wood, called castanets. It is very passionate, fast music which expresses strong emotions.

How to make a flamenco sound

It is easy to produce a typically flamenco sound using the E major chord, shown on the first chord diagram on the right. Strum the chord once. Slide your fingers up one fret and strum again before returning to the first chord.

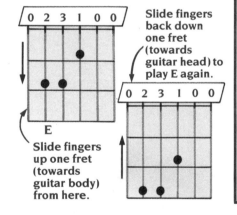

`0 2 3 1 0 0`

E

Slide fingers up one fret (towards guitar body) from here.

Slide fingers back down one fret (towards guitar head) to play E again.

`0 2 3 1 0 0`

Rasguado

Rasguado (pronounced rass-gwah-doh) is a special type of strum associated with flamenco. A simple rasguado involves strumming with your first three fingers one after the other, very quickly. Follow the steps on the right to try it. Keep practising until you can play it really fast.

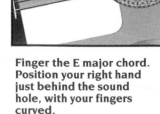

Finger the E major chord. Position your right hand just behind the sound hole, with your fingers curved.

Strum the strings, leading with your third finger. Roll your wrist down away from you to run your other fingers down the strings.

Keep turning your wrist until your fingers are well clear of the strings.

How to play a Spanish strum

The rhythm on the right has a distinctive flamenco feel. Try strumming the rhythm using the chord of A minor. When you have learnt the rhythm, you can find out below how to give it some authentic touches.

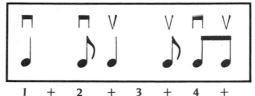

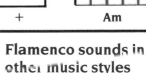

Am

To give the strum a Spanish sound, play the rhythm in Am again, adding a bass note and rasguado. These three pictures show you how.

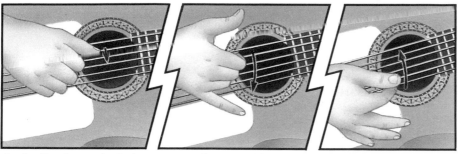

On the first beat, pluck the bass note of the chord (string 5) with your thumb.

Strum the second beat as a rasguado.

Strum the other beats in the normal way with your first finger.

Try this chord sequence, using the Spanish Strum rhythm for each bar.

| Am | G | F | E :‖ |

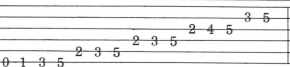

This scale has a typical flamenco sound. Improvise a solo to go with the Am sequence with notes from it.

Flamenco sounds in other music styles

The fast techniques of flamenco have had a great influence upon many bands playing a variety of musical styles. You can hear a flamenco sound in songs like "Spanish Caravan" by The Doors, on their album "Waiting for the Sun" and in many songs by Carlos Santana. Jazz musician John McLaughlin and flamenco guitarist Paco Peña have played tunes together that combine flamenco, jazz and rock sounds.

A flamenco tune to play

Here is a traditional flamenco tune for you to play. It will help you to play fast if, wherever possible, you keep the fingers of your left hand pressed down on the strings, ready to play the next note or chord. For example, you can hold down the second fret on string 4 until the seventh bar. Rasguado the chords in the first and last bars. Pluck the rest of the notes.

This sign means rasguado.

23

Funky guitar

Funky styles, played by artists like James Brown, feature complex rhythms played over a strong beat. You can play typically funky-sounding music using chords called ninths and the techniques shown on this page. The techniques are quite easy, so you can concentrate on building up the rhythms.

Ninth chords

All major chords consist of the first, third and fifth notes of a scale. A ninth chord includes the flattened seventh and ninth notes as well. The ninth note is really the second note of the next octave up. On the right you can see how to play a ninth chord in the key of E. It is called E9.

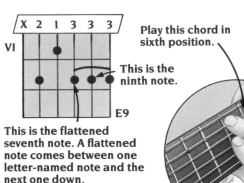

X 2 1 3 3 3

VI

E9

Play this chord in sixth position.

This is the ninth note.

This is the flattened seventh note. A flattened note comes between one letter-named note and the next one down.

It is easy to play lots of ninth chords because the chord shape (the position of your fingers) stays the same. Just move your hand up or down the neck of the guitar. Each chord takes its name from the bass, or lowest, note, fretted by finger 2.

Use finger 3 to cover strings 1, 2 and 3.

The click trick

You can vary the sound of a ninth chord by strumming down and up with your right hand, while your left fingers are lying, but not pressing, on the strings. This technique, called the click, gives the chord a muted, clicking sound used a lot in funky music.

Finger E9 and strum the chord once, then click.

Press fingers down on the strings to strum.

Release pressure and rest fingers on strings to click.

Funky rhythms

You can practise the click (see left) by playing the funky rhythms below. Each rhythm has four beats, each divided into four parts. Say the words written under the rhythms at a steady pace and strum or click on each word with a note above it. You could tap your foot each time you say a number to emphasize the beat, or use a metronome or drum machine (see opposite page). Rhythms 2 and 3 are quite complex but counting the beats should help you get them right.

These two notes are called semi-quavers. Each one lasts for a quarter of a beat.

One beat

One a   and a

Say these words to divide each beat into four parts. Pronounce them "one er and er" and so on.

Count and tap your foot to mark the start of each beat.

This sign shows where you play the click.

1

One a and a two a and a three a and a four a and a

2

One a   and a two a and a three a   and a four a and a

3

One a and a two a and a three a   and a four a and a

This semi-quaver is joined to a dotted quaver. The semi-quaver lasts for a quarter of a beat and the dotted quaver lasts for three-quarters.

24

Sliding chords

You can also alter the sound of a ninth chord by sliding it. Play the ninth chord in fifth position (D#9). As soon as you have played it, keep your fingers pressed down and slide them up one fret to sixth position. This raises the pitch of the chord with a smooth, gliding sound.

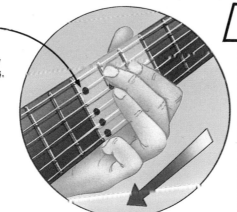

Slide fingers up to position shown by red spots.

Keeping the beat

When practising rhythms, it is vital to keep an even beat. You can play along to a drum machine if you have access to one (read about them on page 38); or you could use a device called a metronome. A digital one, like the one shown here, is quite cheap. It can be set to make a loud, regular clicking. You set it to a pace that suits your speed of playing, so you can fit the right number of strums between each beat.

Using the slide and click together

Use the rhythm below to practise the slide and click techniques. Play the ninth chord in fifth position (D#9).

After playing the first semi-quaver, slide your fingers up to sixth position (E9) to play the rest of the rhythm.

This is a single semi-quaver.

Slide on this quaver. Do not strum.

This is a quaver rest. You do not play anything here.

Say the words if it helps you to get the rhythm right.

One a and a two a and a three a and a four a and a

Playing sharpened ninths

A sharpened ninth is a variation on the ninth chord in which the ninth note is sharpened*. To make sharpened ninths, first finger the ninth chord. Then lift finger 3 so it only presses string 3 and put finger 4 on string 2, one fret higher up the neck. This chord is E sharpened ninth. Played in first position, it is B sharpened ninth. These two sharpened ninth chords feature in the tune on the far right. The tune starts with the two E notes plucked on string 6.

The numbers show the beats in these rhythms.

Use your thumb to pluck these two bass notes on string 6.

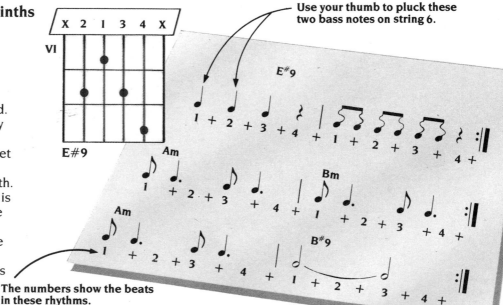

You could record the sequence above on a cassette. Then make up a tune from the notes in the scale of G, shown on the left, to play over the top of it.

7   8   10
7   9   10
7   9   10
7   8   10

Playing classical guitar

Classical guitar style involves plucking individual strings to get clear, crisp notes. It is easier to play this style on a nylon-string acoustic (or Spanish) guitar, due to the way it is strung. On a steel-string acoustic the strings are nearer to each other and on an electric guitar they lie closer to the neck, making it harder to pluck them cleanly.

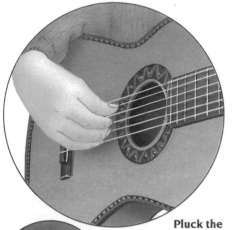

Pluck the strings towards you using your fingernails.

Classical technique

Hold your fingers just behind the sound hole, at right angles to the strings so you can pluck them directly upwards, towards you. This helps to give a full, rich sound. Try not to pull them sideways or the sound will be thinner. You can use either of the plucking techniques shown below. One is the free stroke, used for most classical guitar music. The other is the rest stroke, which gives a stronger, fuller sound.

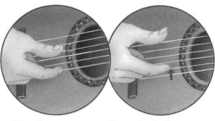

To play a free stroke, pluck the string and lift your finger clear of other strings.

To play a rest stroke, pluck the string towards you and let your finger come to rest on the next string.

Andres Segovia

History of classical guitar

Nylon-string acoustic guitars are often called "classical" because they are associated with classical music. However, early guitars were much smaller than the modern classical guitar.

In the 19th century a Spanish carpenter named Antonio Torres experimented with the design. His new, larger guitars had a better tone, and were used by another Spaniard, Francisco Tarrega, to develop his playing technique. These designs and techniques are still used today.

Andres Segovia, who died in 1987, had a great influence upon modern classical guitar playing. His enthusiasm and expressive technique inspired composers and encouraged players such as John Williams and Julian Bream.

Classical tune

Once you can do both free and rest strokes confidently, listen to the effect they give when you use them to play the classical tune below.

Use rest strokes only on strings 1 and 2, as indicated by this sign.

Hold bass notes for a full bar except where there are two bass notes in the bar.

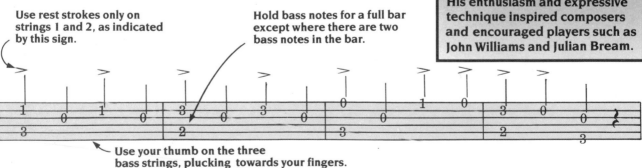

Use your thumb on the three bass strings, plucking towards your fingers.

26

Scales to play

The scale below is in the key of F# major. Play the scale using rest strokes to get a full sound. Use finger 1 to press strings down behind the first fret, finger 2 for the second fret and so on. Playing scales will help improve agility in your fingers.

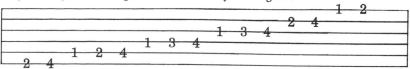

You can use the two rhythms on the right to practise the free stroke, using the index and middle fingers of your right hand alternately to pluck the strings.

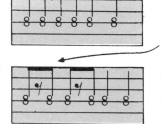

This is a triplet. It is a beat divided into three. The middle count is silent (shown by a rest sign).

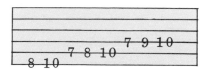

Practise these rhythms on the C major scale on the left. Play the first rhythm on each note of the scale. Then repeat the scale, playing the second rhythm.

Playing ensemble

Classical guitar sounds very powerful when played by two, three, four or more people together. This is called playing ensemble.* You can play the duet below with a friend, each taking a part; or record yourself playing one part first and then play it back and accompany youself with the other part.

Arpeggios

An arpeggio (pronounced are-pej-ee-oh) is a chord in which each note is played separately. It is a technique used a lot in classical guitar accompaniments. Using the chords given here, finger a chord, then pluck the strings in the order shown by the numbers in the purple box below. Use free strokes.

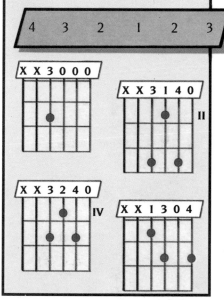

Classical duo

*Ensemble (pronounced on-som-bl) means "together" in French.

Rhythm guitar

Most bands have a rhythm guitarist to keep everyone playing at the same pace. A rhythm guitarist needs to be able to change chords smoothly while keeping the beat.

12 string guitars

Many bands use 12-string guitars to give a jangly quality to their rhythm playing. Hear an electric 12-string on The Byrds' recording of "Mr. Tambourine Man", for instance.

Electric 12-string guitar

The strings lie in pairs tuned to the same note as the equivalent single string.

In the lower four pairs, one string is tuned an octave above the other.

In the top two pairs, the two strings are tuned identically.

Tips on being a good rhythm player

★ Playing your guitar in time with a drum machine or metronome will help you to sustain a steady rhythm, without gradually speeding up or slowing down.

★ Know your chords. Memorize as many as possible. You will need to be familiar with barre chords (see opposite), so you can increase your repertoire.

★ Be aware of your role in the band. The band relies on the rhythm player to provide good, solid backing but not to dominate by playing too loudly.

★ You can emphasize a rhythm by using your left hand to damp each chord. This makes a beat rather than a musical sound. (Damping is described on page 20.)

A rhythm solo to play

Here is the rhythm for the song at the bottom of the page. Practise it on the Am chord, strumming the second beat in arpeggio style (see previous page), so that individual notes of the chord can be heard.

These two chords, used in the song below, are typical of the power chords played by Pete Townshend of The Who. Play the chords in the rhythm shown in the song.

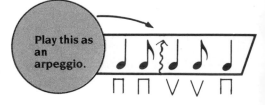

Play this as an arpeggio.

The E sus (suspended) 4 chord includes the fourth note of the E major scale.

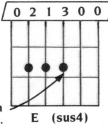

0	2	1	3	0	0

E   (sus4)

0	2	3	1	0	0

E

The House of the Rising Sun

Am   C   D   F
There is a house in New Orleans
Am   C   Esus 4   E
They call the Rising Sun, ⌣

Change to this rhythm to play the power chords.

Am   C   D   F
And it's been the ruin of many a poor boy,
Am   E   Am   Esus 4
And God, I know I'm one. ⌣

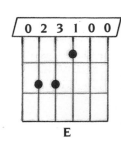

Barre chords

Barre chords are chord shapes that can be played in any position on the neck, with finger 1 pressing across the strings like a bar. The two most common types of barre chords are called primary and secondary. Once you know the shapes to finger for them, you can move up and down the neck of the guitar and play any chord you like.

Primary barre chords

To play primary barre chords, finger 1 stretches across all six strings.

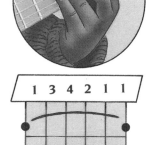

To play a major chord, place your other fingers in the shape shown in the picture and chord diagram on the right. You can play any major chord by moving your fingers in this shape, up or down the guitar neck.

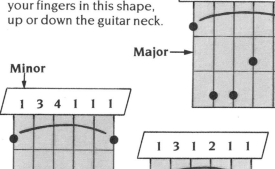

Major →

Minor ↓

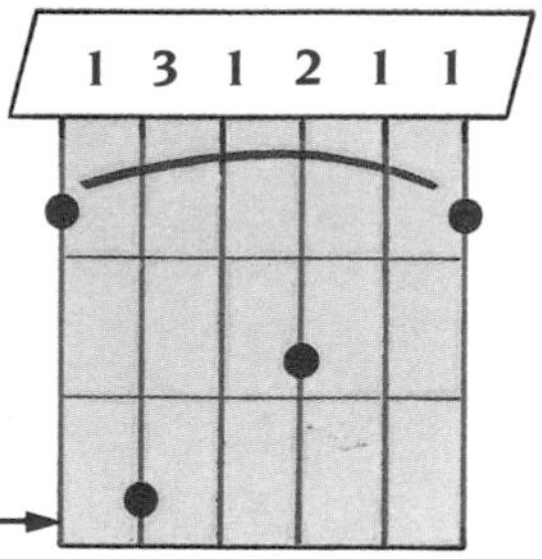

7th →

*There is more about changing keys on page 37.

Using barre chords

Barre chords make it easy to change the key of a song.* Try playing "The House of the Rising Sun" again, using barre chords to play it in the key of Em, as shown below. Use primary and secondary barre chords as indicated by the Roman numerals.

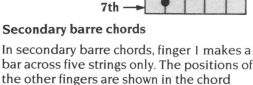

The House of the Rising Sun

| Em | G | A | C | Em | G | B₇ | ⅞ |

II   I   I   II   II   I   I

Play a **secondary** barre chord. ← → Play a **primary** barre chord.

| Em | G | A | C | Em | B₇ | Em | ⅞ :‖ |

II   I   I   II   II   I   II

◄ You can make minor and seventh chords in the same way. Place your fingers in the correct shape, as shown on the chord diagrams on the left. Then move your hand up and down the neck to play different chords.

Each chord takes its name from the bass note, made by finger 1 pressing on string 6. For example, if you play these chords in third position, the bass note is G and the chord is G major, G minor or G seventh.

Secondary barre chords

In secondary barre chords, finger 1 makes a bar across five strings only. The positions of the other fingers are shown in the chord diagrams on the right. This time the chord is named after the note made by finger 1 on string 5.

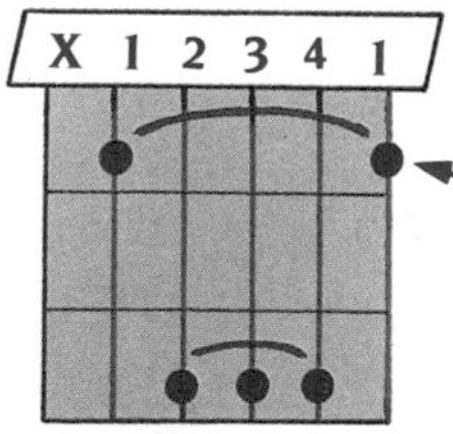

This picture shows the position of the fingers for the major chord shape. Use just finger 3 as a bar across strings 4, 3 and 2, if you prefer.

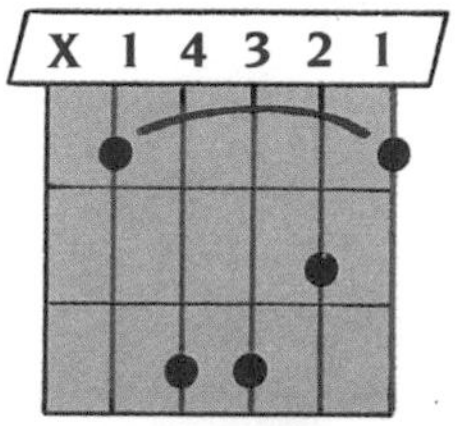

Major

If you play this chord in first position, the bass note is B♭ and the chord is B♭ major.

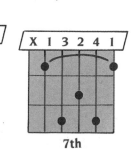

Minor   **7th**

Rhythm guitarists use barre chords a lot because they often need to make many quick chord changes. Every chord can be played either as a primary or a secondary barre chord. If you use both types you can avoid having to make big leaps up and down the neck of the guitar to change chords, so you can play faster.

29

Jazz

Jazz guitarists usually like to improvise and try out new rhythms and harmonies. To do this, you need to be familiar with chords and scales, so that you can experiment with giving them a jazz style. You can find out how to play some jazz chords and tunes below.

Playing jazz chords

You can give chords a jazz sound by adding a note. Add the seventh note of the scale to secondary barre chords to make major and minor seventh chords (see right). You can play these chord shapes anywhere on the guitar neck. They are named after their bass note.

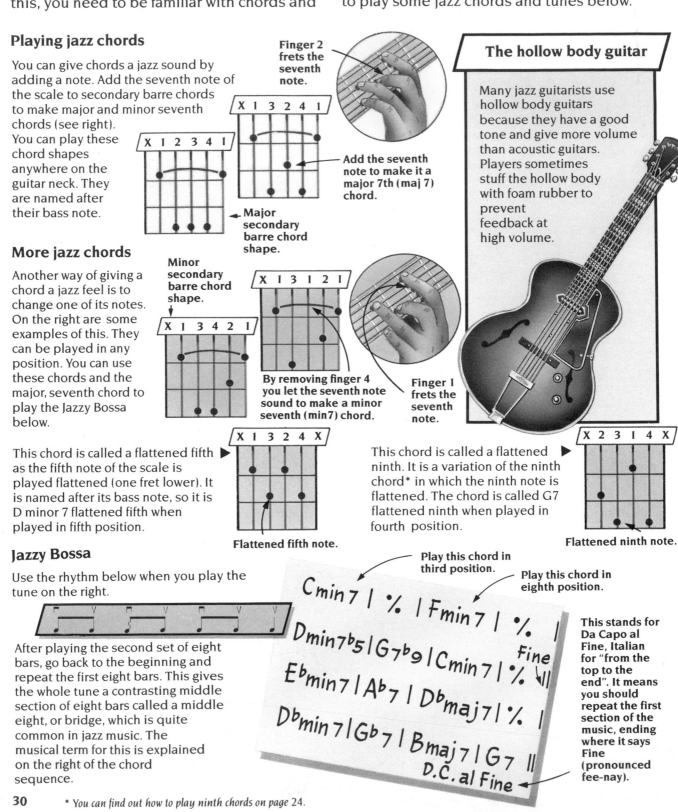

Finger 2 frets the seventh note.

X 1 3 2 4 1

Add the seventh note to make it a major 7th (maj 7) chord.

X 1 2 3 4 1

◄ Major secondary barre chord shape.

The hollow body guitar

Many jazz guitarists use hollow body guitars because they have a good tone and give more volume than acoustic guitars. Players sometimes stuff the hollow body with foam rubber to prevent feedback at high volume.

More jazz chords

Another way of giving a chord a jazz feel is to change one of its notes. On the right are some examples of this. They can be played in any position. You can use these chords and the major, seventh chord to play the Jazzy Bossa below.

Minor secondary barre chord shape.

X 1 3 4 2 1

X 1 3 1 2 1

By removing finger 4 you let the seventh note sound to make a minor seventh (min7) chord.

Finger 1 frets the seventh note.

This chord is called a flattened fifth ▶ as the fifth note of the scale is played flattened (one fret lower). It is named after its bass note, so it is D minor 7 flattened fifth when played in fifth position.

X 1 3 2 4 X

Flattened fifth note.

This chord is called a flattened ▶ ninth. It is a variation of the ninth chord* in which the ninth note is flattened. The chord is called G7 flattened ninth when played in fourth position.

X 2 3 1 4 X

Flattened ninth note.

Jazzy Bossa

Use the rhythm below when you play the tune on the right.

After playing the second set of eight bars, go back to the beginning and repeat the first eight bars. This gives the whole tune a contrasting middle section of eight bars called a middle eight, or bridge, which is quite common in jazz music. The musical term for this is explained on the right of the chord sequence.

Play this chord in third position.

Play this chord in eighth position.

Cmin 7 | % | Fmin 7 | % |
Dmin 7 $\flat$5 | G7 $\flat$9 | Cmin 7 | % | Fine
E$\flat$min 7 | A$\flat$7 | D$\flat$maj 7 | % |
D$\flat$min 7 | G$\flat$7 | Bmaj 7 | G7 ‖
D.C. al Fine

This stands for Da Capo al Fine, Italian for "from the top to the end". It means you should repeat the first section of the music, ending where it says Fine (pronounced fee-nay).

* You can find out how to play ninth chords on page 24.

Scales

In order to improvise a jazz solo, you need to be familiar with scales.* There are two main kinds of scales, major and minor. You can play a scale in any position on the guitar neck. The note you start on will tell you the name of the key the scale is in.

Major scale

This diagram shows the notes of the major scale over two octaves. To play it, start on string 6, on any fret. Play all the notes on string 6, then those on string 5, 4 and so on. Start at the lower end of the neck each time you change strings. If you start on C (at the eighth fret), it is the scale of C major.

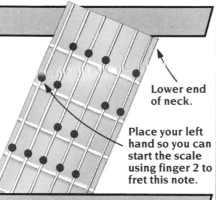

Lower end of neck.

Place your left hand so you can start the scale using finger 2 to fret this note.

Minor scale

Start the scale by using finger 4 to fret this note.

Slide finger 4 up one fret to play this note. All your fingers then move up one position to finish playing the scale.

A minor scale sounds different to a major scale because the distance between some of the notes is different. Like a minor chord, it has a sad quality. Start again on any fret on string 6 and play all the notes on one string before moving on to the next. If you play the scale in fifth position, the first note is C and the scale is C minor.

Jazz scale exercise

Now try this major scale exercise, which will help you practise string-crossing, as described on page 14. The scale consists of a series of triplets. Each triplet is made up of three consecutive notes of the scale. You can repeat the scale in any position by playing the notes in a similar pattern of triplets.

The middle note of each triplet begins the next one.

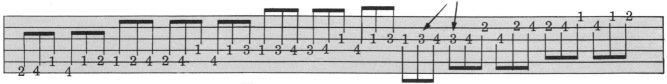

Improvising a jazz lead

You can use notes from the scales above to improvise a jazz solo over a chord sequence in a major or minor key, such as the one on the right. Choose notes in the same key as the chord sequence. Record the chord sequence to accompany yourself.

```
Cmaj7 | ∕. | Dmin7 | ∕. |
Emin7 | Fmaj7 | Cmaj7 | ∕. ‖    Fine
Cmin7 | ∕. | Fmin7 | ∕. |
Dmin7♭5 | G7♭9 | Cmin7 | G7 ‖
                        D.C. al Fine
```

Use the C major scale to improvise through the first eight bars and the C minor scale for the rest. Listen to some jazz, such as Sade or Wes Montgomery, to get some ideas for improvising.

* There is more about scales on page 12.

History of jazz guitar

Jazz started in New Orleans, in the USA, at around the turn of the twentieth century. Musicians started to improvise tunes based on African rhythms and spiritual songs, turning them into catchy dance tunes.

The guitar did not begin to feature in jazz bands until the 1920s, when arch-top acoustic guitars were developed. These had an arched shape and steel strings, which enabled them to produce enough volume to be heard against all the other instruments in a jazz band. At first they were mainly used in the place of banjos for playing rhythm, because a greater variety of chords could be played on a guitar.

As semi-acoustic and electric guitars developed, jazz bands began to use them for melody and solo playing as well. Jazz guitar has increased in popularity and nowadays many different kinds of bands, such as rock and folk, include jazz styles in their repertoire.

Electric bass guitar

The electric bass was developed in the 1950s to replace the double bass. Its four strings are tuned to the same notes as a double bass, one octave below the lower four strings on an ordinary guitar. The bass works with drums and rhythm guitar to provide rhythmic backing and is also used for playing melody. You can play bass lines on any guitar (using the lower four strings only), but they sound best on a bass.

Harmonics

Harmonics are extra notes, made by playing the strings in a special way, which sound particularly good on bass guitars. They have a clear, bell-like quality that you can use as a special effect.

Playing harmonics

You can play harmonics on many frets, but they work best at the fifth, seventh and twelfth frets. Play one on the twelfth fret of any string, as shown below. It is one octave higher than the open string.

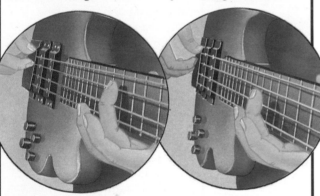

Use finger 2 lightly to touch a string directly over a fret while you pluck it. Do not press down on the string.

As soon as you have played the note, remove finger 2 from the string. You will then hear the harmonic note.

Tuning the bass

Using harmonics is a more accurate way of tuning a bass guitar than the fifth fret method. Harmonic notes are purer than open string notes on strings tuned to a lower octave.

To tune a bass, play a harmonic on each pair of strings in turn, at the frets indicated below. Adjust the machine head of the higher string, if necessary, until they sound the same. Remember that string 4 is the lowest string on a bass guitar.

Fifth fret string 4 = Seventh fret string 3.

Fifth fret string 3 = Seventh fret string 2.

Fifth fret string 2 = Seventh fret string 1.

A simple bass line

You can play a simple bass accompaniment by using the key note of each chord being played on a rhythm guitar or keyboard. Below is a chord sequence with a bass line for you to try. The string chart for the bass part has only four lines, representing the four strings of the bass guitar*.

One person plays the chords while the other plays the bass line. The bassist can either play each note once, or use the pop bass rhythm given for each bar.

The keyboards player or rhythm guitarist plays these chords.

These notes form the bass line.

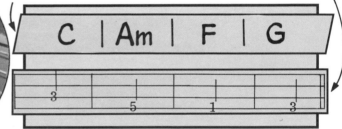

C | Am | F | G

Use the first two fingers of your right hand alternately, to pluck the strings for the bass line. Use the rest stroke shown on page 26.

Play this rhythm for each bar.

Pop bass rhythm.

Developing a bass line

You can add notes between the key notes to develop a bass line. This helps lead smoothly from one note to another, as well as being more interesting. On the bass line below, pluck the key notes with your index finger and the notes in between, which are called passing notes, with your middle finger.

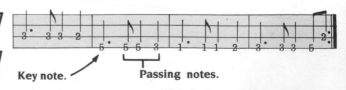

Key note.   **Passing notes.**

*To remind yourself how to read string charts see page 12.

Bass styles

There are typical reggae and funky bass styles for you to try on this page. To develop your own style, try accompanying the chord sequences in this book. Experiment with passing notes to build up good-sounding bass lines.

Reggae bass

The main features of a reggae bass line are a steady beat and a deep tone. These are more important than the number of notes you play. The bass line below can be played with Joshua Fit the Battle of Jericho on page 21. If you are using an ordinary electric guitar, turn the bass amplifier to full bass with no treble, to get a good deep sound.

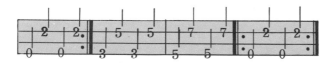

Funky bass

You can play this funky bass line with the chord sequence in E on page 25. Use your thumb to play the notes on string 4 (lowest string) and your middle fingers for the others.

Classical bass guitar

A recent development is a special six-string acoustic bass used in classical guitar ensembles. All six strings are metal covered, the neck is one fret longer and it is tuned to an octave below normal guitar pitch.

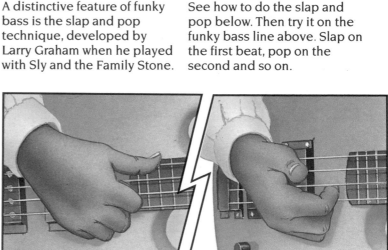

Bass guitar strings

There are two common types of bass strings. Roundwound bass strings are wound with wire and give a bright sound suitable for most styles. Flatwound strings are wrapped with flat tape and give a smoother sound preferred by jazz guitarists.

Great guitarists – Stanley Clarke

The American bassist, Stanley Clarke, has helped increase the bass's popularity by using it for playing solos as well as rhythms. He plays a blend of styles including classical, jazz and rock, with a plucking technique that gives his music an interesting treble sound.

The "slap and pop"

A distinctive feature of funky bass is the slap and pop technique, developed by Larry Graham when he played with Sly and the Family Stone.

See how to do the slap and pop below. Then try it on the funky bass line above. Slap on the first beat, pop on the second and so on.

Slap down on string 4 with the side of your thumb so that the string hits the frets.

Then hook your first finger under string 2 and pull up to make a popping sound.

Two Blues Tunes

Here are two blues tunes which feature new, more advanced rhythms. You can play each tune using just one chord shape, played in different positions and interspersed with bass notes. Use the vibrato technique on the next page to add more expression.

The seventh chord

This chord shape can be played anywhere on the neck of the guitar. It is called a seventh because it includes the seventh note of the scale. You can use it in different positions to play the chords in the blues tune below. The chord is C7 when played in first position because the bass note is C.

This is called the seventh note. ▶

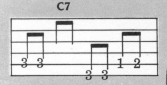

X   3   2   4   1   X

This note is C.

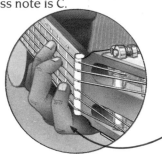

Play only the middle four strings. To avoid playing string 1, let finger 1 lie lightly on it so that if you play it by mistake, it does not sound.

The Lazy Blues

Now use the chords to play the Lazy Blues. Like other 12-bar blues patterns, the last bar is different. You can improvise an ending of your own, if you prefer.

Blues rhythm

Below is the pattern of chords and single notes for the Lazy Blues (below, left). Play the rhythm on the C7 chord, using downstrokes only and a plectrum, if you have one. You can change quickly between single notes and chords by positioning your left hand fingers for the chord, while you play the bass note, as shown below.

C7

3 3
      3 3   1 2

Use finger 3 to fret the bass note and pluck the string twice. Keep finger 3 pressed down.

While you are plucking the string, move your other left fingers into position ready to play the C7 chord that follows.

Repeat the rhythm, playing the seventh chord in sixth and eighth position (F7 and G7).

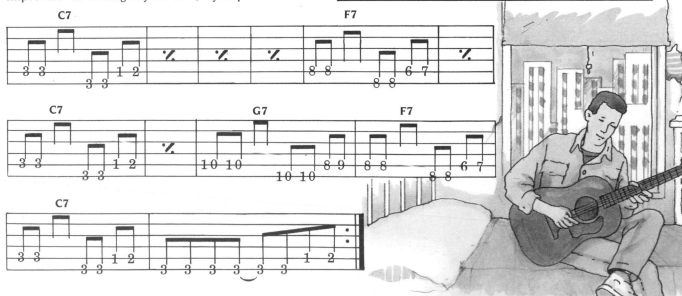

34

Jazzing up the ninth chord

You use the ninth chord (see page 25) in the Jazzy City Blues below. Practise strumming the chord in fourth and sixth positions, alternating the bass note as shown on this chord diagram.

Use finger 2 to alternate the bass note between strings 5 and 6.

These two beats are triplets. Count in threes, as shown, to divide each beat into three. Playing the triplets should sound like the boogie rhythm on page 10.

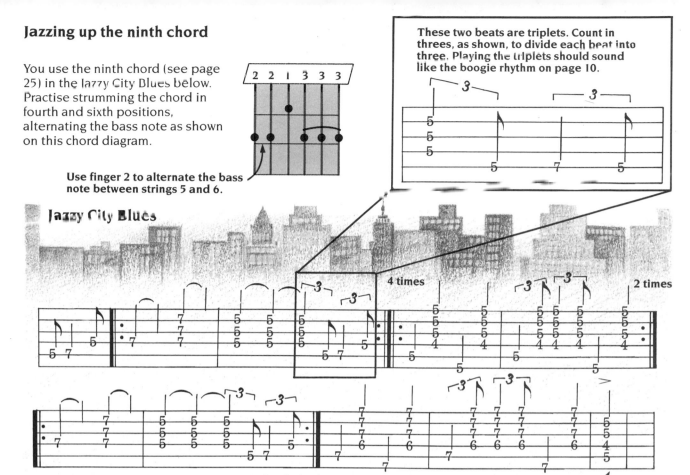

Jazzy City Blues

To finish this bar and the next one, play improvised notes from the blues scale in fifth position before returning to the beginning.

Playing vibrato

Vibrato is a musical term meaning a vibrating note. Using vibrato helps put feeling into a tune. There are two ways you can do it, as shown on the right. Try both and use whichever you find easier.

Method 1. Press down on a string with a left hand finger and rock your wrist as you play the note.

Method 2. Move the string quickly up and down with your finger as you play the note.

You could record the Lazy Blues or the Jazzy City Blues and then improvise from the blues scale over the top. Use vibrato on some notes, such as at the beginning of each bar. Try bending some strings, too, for a change.*

The best position in which to play vibrato depends on your guitar's action (the height of the strings above the neck). On an electric or nylon-string acoustic guitar with a high action, vibrato is easier to play, and sounds better, in positions higher up the neck. If you are playing a low-action, steel-string acoustic, vibrato works best lower down the neck.

Train whistle trick

A popular blues trick is to slide a chord to sound like an American train whistle. Get a friend to play the rhythm below on open string 6. Meanwhile, play a two-string chord, sliding down and up a fret as you play.

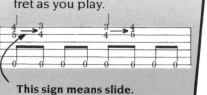

This sign means slide.

The string-bending technique is described on page 15.

Further ways of using chords

It is useful to be familiar with several chord sets (see below) so that you can play tunes based on the 3-chord trick in different keys. Playing a tune in a new key is called transposing. If the tune has several chord changes you will probably find it easier to use barre chords to transpose, as shown opposite. The bass runs described here help make your chord changes smoother.

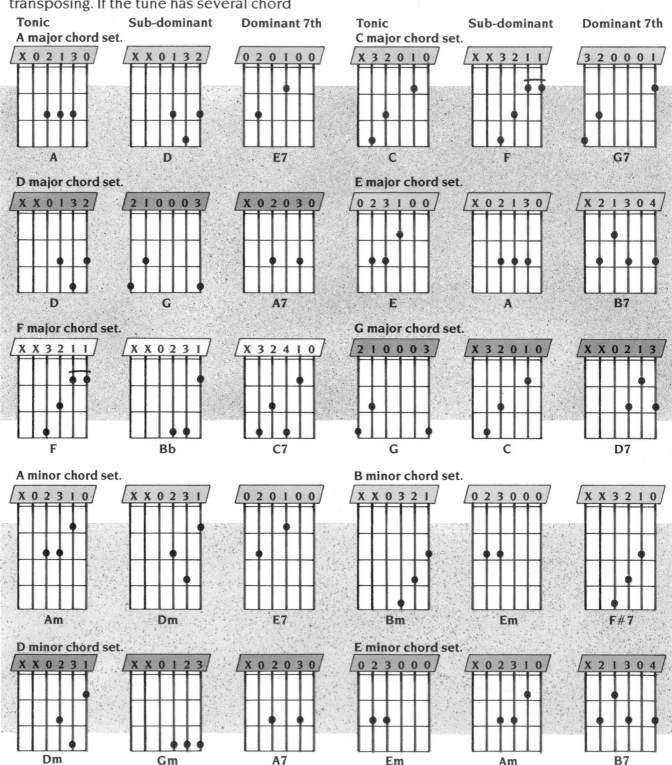

Tonic	Sub-dominant	Dominant 7th	Tonic	Sub-dominant	Dominant 7th

A major chord set. / C major chord set.

- X 0 2 1 3 0 — A
- X X 0 1 3 2 — D
- 0 2 0 1 0 0 — E7
- X 3 2 0 1 0 — C
- X X 3 2 1 1 — F
- 3 2 0 0 0 1 — G7

D major chord set. / E major chord set.

- X X 0 1 3 2 — D
- 2 1 0 0 0 3 — G
- X 0 2 0 3 0 — A7
- 0 2 3 1 0 0 — E
- X 0 2 1 3 0 — A
- X 2 1 3 0 4 — B7

F major chord set. / G major chord set.

- X X 3 2 1 1 — F
- X X 0 2 3 1 — Bb
- X 3 2 4 1 0 — C7
- 2 1 0 0 0 3 — G
- X 3 2 0 1 0 — C
- X X 0 2 1 3 — D7

A minor chord set. / B minor chord set.

- X 0 2 3 1 0 — Am
- X X 0 2 3 1 — Dm
- 0 2 0 1 0 0 — E7
- X X 0 3 2 1 — Bm
- 0 2 3 0 0 0 — Em
- X X 3 2 1 0 — F#7

D minor chord set. / E minor chord set.

- X X 0 2 3 1 — Dm
- X X 0 1 2 3 — Gm
- X 0 2 0 3 0 — A7
- 0 2 3 0 0 0 — Em
- X 0 2 3 1 0 — Am
- X 2 1 3 0 4 — B7

Transposing tunes using barre chords

You can use primary and secondary barre chords* to play a tune in a different key by the following method.

1. Work out how many frets there are between the original key and the new key. Use the picture of the guitar neck on page 18 to help you, if you like. Count the number of frets between the two bass notes of the two key chords along one string of the guitar.

2. Count up or down the same number of frets to find the new name for each chord in the tune.

3. Find the key note of each new chord on string 5 or 6, as near to the middle of the neck as you can, using the picture on page 18 again. This gives the position for the chord to be played in primary (if the key note is on string 6) or secondary (if the key note is on string 5) barre form. Use whichever form involves the smallest change in hand position from the previous chord.

The example below shows how to transpose the three chord set in G up to the key of G#. The chords G, C and D become G#, C# and D#. By changing between primary and secondary barre chords you can play the three chords very close to each other on the guitar neck, as shown in the pictures.

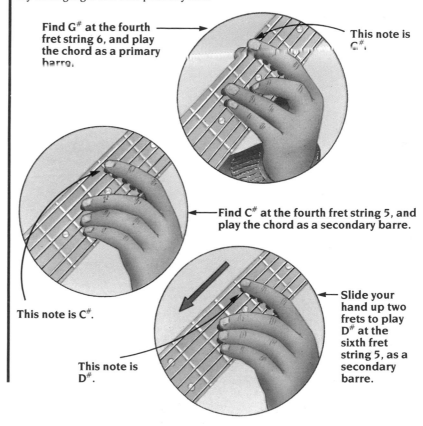

Find G# at the fourth fret string 6, and play the chord as a primary barre.

This note is G#.

Find C# at the fourth fret string 5, and play the chord as a secondary barre.

This note is C#.

This note is D#.

Slide your hand up two frets to play D# at the sixth fret string 5, as a secondary barre.

Bass runs

A bass run is a series of notes which links the bass notes of two chords. It is a technique used a lot in folk music, where you pluck bass notes to provide your own backing rhythms. In the example below, each chord is linked to the next by two notes, one of which is plucked on an open string. This makes the whole sequence more interesting and flowing. It also allows you more time to position your fingers ready to play the next chord, making the chord changes smoother. Practise the sequence, playing each chord as a bass/chord strum. You could then repeat the Country Strum on page 9 with bass runs.

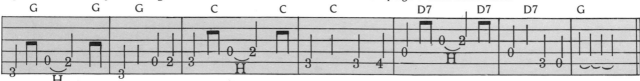

Bass runs sound particularly effective when combined with hammer-ons, as in the sequence below. You could vary the sequence by changing the pattern of strums and adding more hammer-ons. Then try working out bass runs for other chord sets, again using combinations of open and fretted notes that come between the two bass notes.

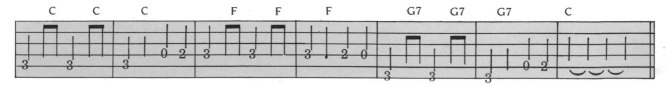

* The different barre chord shapes are shown on page 29.

Special effects

You can create a number of special effects by using the equipment and playing techniques described on these two pages. Some of these alter the sound of the guitar. Others, such as the drum machine, can add to or help you to improve your playing. They are quite easy to use with a bit of practice and can add a variety of new sounds to your repertoire.

Special effects boxes

You can create some interesting sounds on an electric guitar by using pedal-operated effects boxes. Each box alters the sound of your playing in a particular way. If you only want to use one effects box at a time, you can plug it in between your guitar and the amplifier, as shown in the picture on the right.

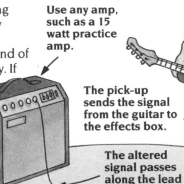

Use any amp, such as a 15 watt practice amp.

The pick-up sends the signal from the guitar to the effects box.

The altered signal passes along the lead to the amp.

Push down on the pedal with your foot.

Most amps used by professional guitarists have "send and return" sockets so that you can use several pedal-operated effects linked together on one loop. Some of the available effects are described around the picture below.

Guitar lead

The effects box alters the signal.

One special effects box only.

Distortion

A distortion box imitates the raw, distorted sound produced by early amps when they were turned up loud. It gives a special "rock'n'roll" feel to the music.

Chorus

The chorus effect acts to make the sound of the guitar fuller and richer. You can adjust the depth of the chorus to the amount you want.

Digital delay

Digital delay units give music an echoing sound, called delay. They can make complex delay patterns that fade out over any length of time you choose.

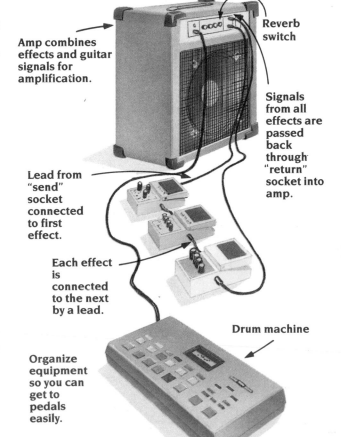

Amp combines effects and guitar signals for amplification.

Reverb switch

Signals from all effects are passed back through "return" socket into amp.

Lead from "send" socket connected to first effect.

Each effect is connected to the next by a lead.

Organize equipment so you can get to pedals easily.

Drum machine

Other effects

Reverb

The reverberation (reverb) effect is usually built into guitar amps and operated by a switch. It makes a note sound as if it is played in an empty room. It is sometimes used as a separate effect in recording studios to enrich the sound after recording is complete.

The drum machine

A drum machine plugs into an amp. It produces rhythms of varying complexity, depending on the type of machine. Some can be programmed with your own rhythms. A drum machine can help you practise your rhythm and timing. A band may use one instead of a drummer, although some people think it creates a rather soulless beat.

Tremolo arm

A tremolo arm alters the pitch of a note to make a wavering sound. On most guitars you can fit one to the front, but it is built into some models, such as the Fender Stratocaster. Tremolo was used a lot in the 1960s by bands like The Beach Boys and is still used when bands want to re-create a 60s sound.

Press arm down to lower pitch of note. Pull arm up to return note to original pitch.

The capo

A capo (pronounced cap-oh) is a clamp that fits across the fingerboard of an acoustic or electric guitar. It reduces the length of the string you play and so raises the pitch of the note. Playing with a capo on will put a tune in a higher key without you having to alter the chords. This is especially useful if you play folk music as you can keep the folky sound of the open-string chords instead of playing barre chords (see page 29).

This guitar has a capo ▶ fitted. Starting at the nut end, each fret raises the pitch by one semi-tone. If you clamp the capo behind the third fret, a C major chord becomes Eb major.

Capo behind third fret raises each note by three semi-tones.

Effects specialists – Adrian Belew

Adrian Belew has experimented a lot with special effects. He invented a variety of new effects in his work with bands such as Talking Heads. Try listening to his solo album "Lone Rhinoceros" to hear a great display of effects.

Joe Walsh

Joe Walsh used some unique effects when he played with The Eagles. These included running a plectrum sideways down between the fifth and sixth strings, with one of its edges touching each string, to produce a screeching, downwards-sliding note.

Jan Akkerman

Jan Akkerman, who played with the Dutch band Focus, had a way of producing a sound like a violin from his electric guitar. He played a note while the volume on the guitar was off and then used the little finger of his right hand to turn the volume on again, straight after playing. This is quite tricky to do, but with practice you should be able to try it for yourself.

Sliding notes

You can give a note a bluesy sound by sliding a left finger up or down between the notes as you play a string. Try this effect as an introduction to a blues solo in fifth position by sliding finger 3 along from the third fret to the eighth fret on string 6.

Some capos ▶ are clamped on by a spring mechanism; others are held in position by a nylon strap.

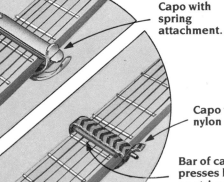

Capo with spring attachment.

Capo with nylon strap.

Bar of capo presses hard on strings.

Recording at home

You can get a good idea of what you or your band really sound like by recording yourselves. You can experiment with ideas for songs; then listen critically to see if you need to improve your material. If you plan to go further in the music business, you will need to make a demonstration (demo) tape to show your ability. It is possible to make good recordings at home, as described here.

Recording on cassette

The cheapest and simplest way to make a recording is on a standard portable cassette recorder. Put the machine in the middle of the room, plug in a microphone (mic or mike, for short) and start playing.

Recording tips

For better-quality recordings, such as demo tapes (see below), use a high-fidelity (hi-fi) recorder which will reproduce the sound you make with greater precision and clarity.

A machine called a mixer* lets you adjust, or "mix", the volume and tone of instruments as you record. Here are some tips for using this equipment:

★ Use good quality leads and chrome tape.
★ Keep tape heads clean.
★ Use high output (powerful) mikes for maximum tape saturation.
★ When recording acoustic instruments, soundproof the room. Heavy curtains, rugs on walls and thick carpets help "deaden" unwanted noises.
★ If you are recording more than one instrument, adjust the tone and volume so lead instruments and voices are loudest.

Demo tapes

Groups usually make a demo tape to send to people who may be able to help them get work or recording contracts. It is vital to make the best quality tape you can. It should show your style and range, so use your own songs if possible. Stick labels on tapes and boxes, clearly marked with your name, song titles and date. Some community centres have recording facilities and may help you make a demo.

Portable studios

One of the best ways to make home recordings is on a portable multi-track recording studio. You can use it to compose or arrange tunes and experiment with instruments and effects.

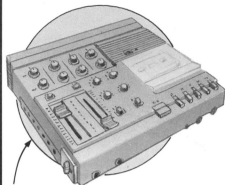

A portable studio combines a cassette recorder and mixer.

Four separate tracks enable you to record different instrumental and vocal parts and combine them on one tape.

Portable studios are expensive to buy* but they can be hired quite cheaply. A school or youth club may have one you could borrow.

It helps to wear "cans" (headphones) when you record or play back the tape. Plug them into the mixer, listen to the input and adjust the mix.

Volume and tone controls

A stand brings the mike close to the instruments.

The mixer is plugged between the mike and recorder. You use it to balance the input from instruments and mix it down to stereo before feeding it into the recorder.

Use a mains-powered hi-fi because batteries give a fluctuating current that may cause sound distortion.

Set the input selector switch to the line/mic position when recording. Set it to remix when playing the tape back and adjusting the mix.

Wear cans to listen to yourself playing.

Guitar lead plugs into studio.

The recorder can combine the first three tracks onto the fourth, as you record it (known as bouncing), so they are free for more recording.

This is an outboard effects processor. If you connect it to the recorder you can add effects, such as reverb on voices or chorus on guitars.

Cassette recorder connected to portable studio.

Tips

★ Record at a high volume level to overcome tape background noise.

★ Record a count-in of four beats so you start each track at the same place.

★ If using a drum machine, record another instrument (such as bass guitar) at the same time.

Some portable studios work on batteries, too, so you can record a "notebook" of your ideas anywhere, including out of doors.

Using a portable studio

Below is a recommended order for recording several instruments. Some you might use are suggested, but the order is the same even if all parts are played on guitar (see solo project, below).

Track 1. Rhythm: bass guitar, drums.
Track 2. Melody: backing, such as keyboards, acoustic guitar.
Track 3. Lead: lead guitar.
Track 4. Extras: vocals, other instruments.

★ Record the tracks one at a time.
★ Listen to previous tracks through headphones while recording a new track.
★ Play back the completed tape on the remix switch on your recorder to hear what it is like.
★ Adjust the volume of the tracks until the balance of instruments and voices is right.
★ Copy the tape onto a cassette recorder. This combines the four tracks into two (stereo).

The final version is a mastertape, from which you can make copies.

Solo project

Here is how to record a boogie song in a typical "A B A" arrangement, in which the melody is replaced by a lead solo in the middle section of the song. This arrangement is shown on the right. You could use it as a starting point for recording your own ideas.

★ Track 1 (rhythm). Give a four beat count-in, then play the 12-bar blues in the boogie rhythm (see page 12) three times.

★ Track 2 (melody). Record the melody on the right. Play it once, leave the next 12 bars blank, then repeat.

★ Track 3 (lead). Improvise a lead solo from the blues scale on the middle 12 bars.

★ Track 4 (voice). Add a voice, more percussion or another instrument. You could bounce the other tracks at the same time and record more tracks.

Track	A	B	A
1	Rhythm	Rhythm	Rhythm
2	Melody		Melody
3		Lead	
4	Voice	Voice	Voice

Playing in a band

Playing the guitar can give you good opportunities for joining a band, as most bands include guitars in their line-up. Many groups prefer to play one particular style, so join one whose tastes coincide with yours. For most bands, playing live is essential so they become known. Here are some tips on setting up a band and performing.

Forming a band

Most people start playing with friends or join a local band. The personal notices page in a local paper or magazine is a good place to look for bands who want a musician with your skills or to advertise for a band to play in; or try the noticeboard of a community centre or music shop.

Successful rehearsing

For rehearsals you need to find a room that is large enough to hold all your equipment and where you will not disturb other people. You may be able to hire a room in a community centre or recording studio. Allow plenty of rehearsal time to prepare for a performance.

Making the most of rehearsals
★ Be prepared to work with a leader and accept his or her decisions.
★ Learn your own part beforehand.
★ Turn up on time and be available for the length of the rehearsal.
★ Play on even if you make a mistake, so as not to interrupt the song.
★ Get used to a microphone. If you sing, the mike must stay close to your mouth as you move your head.

Building up a repertoire

You need about two dozen songs in your repertoire (the songs you perform). Let all the band have a go at writing them and vary the styles so as not to be boring. You can also play your own versions of other people's songs. Avoid on-stage debate by deciding your choice and order of songs before a performance.

Auditions

Any musician wanting to join a band can expect to be given a try-out, or audition. Here are some of the things people look out for to see whether someone is suitable.

★ The ability to pick up tunes easily.
★ A good sense of rhythm.
★ Some original material to contribute.
★ A personality that will fit in with the rest of the band.

Before you audition someone, invite them to meet the other band members. You could give them a tape to listen to of the sort of music you like to play, to see if it suits their style too. When auditioning, ask them to join in whatever you are playing to get an idea of their musical ability.

Keep your mouth quite close to the mike.

★ Stand where you can see and hear each other playing. You should work as a team, listening to each other and exchanging ideas.
★ Practise between rehearsals. Try an idea for a song and see what the band thinks next time.

Watch and listen to each other.

Your choice of guitar can add to your image.

Having an image

Many things can contribute to your band's visual impact, or image: your musical style, clothes, the name of your band, your stage lay-out and lighting and so on. You don't have to consciously develop an image. The band's image will be most successful if it grows out of the music you play and reflects your real personalities. An image that is not natural is easily seen through.

Tips for getting started

★ Play at friends' parties.
★ Talk to musicians. At gigs, ask the band how they got started.
★ Ask in libraries or arts centres for lists of clubs and events.
★ Find out what music clubs specialize in and ask if they would like you to play. Be ready to submit a demo tape.
★ Prepare a few songs for audition that show your range and style.

Preparing for a gig

Having booked a venue, hire a PA if necessary. To avoid problems of distortion, it should be powerful enough for you not to have to run it at full capacity. Plan transport to the gig in advance. You may need a small van to carry all your gear.

Publicity

To get as large an audience as possible, advertise your gig in advance. Print your own posters, detailing information such as:

Venue and date.

Entrance fee.

Where to buy tickets.

If you can, display posters in record shops and venues where music similar to yours is played. Ask friends to display them, too. Try to get into venues listings in magazines, by contacting the listings editor. Someone from the magazine may be sent to review the gig if you send them a couple of free tickets.

Fees

Play for a fee, however small, if you can or you will undermine the value of your performance. At first, you may have to pay for the venue and take the money from ticket sales as payment.

Tickets

Make tickets and number them so you know how many sell. Price them in line with other bands in your area. Ask record shops if they will sell some for you and get a friend to sell them at the venue. A "float" of money will be needed, to give change.

Performance tips

★ Get people's attention by starting with a catchy tune with a strong beat.
★ Keep introductions to songs short.
★ Vary the pace, grouping songs of a similar style in twos or threes.
★ If you want people to dance, play well-known dance tunes.
★ If you are warming up for another band, work the audience up into a receptive mood. Make your last song really good so you, too, are remembered.
★ Be ready to alter your set (programme) according to audience reaction.
★ If you want an encore, play fast, exciting songs at the end to get the audience in the mood for applauding. Prepare a couple of songs for your encore or repeat your best ones.

Before the performance

1. Get to the venue in time to set up the equipment* carefully so the audience will hear the best sound possible.
2. Do a sound check (see below).
3. Arrange equipment so the audience can see the whole band.
4. Have some towels for wiping instruments and your hands.

5. Allow instruments to warm up under stage lights. Tune them just before the audience arrives, then leave the stage.
6. Turn house lights down to get people's attention. Then come on stage and start playing. Note that you probably will not be able to see your audience in the dark.

Mark levels on the mixer.

Adjusting the sound

The sound you hear on stage will be different from what the audience hears. Place the mixer out in front of the stage and get the sound mixer (or a friend who knows how to use it) to control the mix and adjust it to deal with feedback (see next page).

Do a sound check before the show. Play a song and adjust the volume and tone levels, marking the levels on the mixer.

The audience will affect the acoustics, so adjust the sound level as you play.

*See the next two pages.

Equipment for performance

If you are going to play in public, you need to increase the sound you produce so that you can be clearly heard by your audience. You will probably need some extra equipment to do this, especially to play at large venues. The equipment described here is what an electric or acoustic guitarist needs, from the minimum basics to a more advanced system. In a band, the other instruments will also need amplification.

Microphones

If you play in a club or larger venue, you will need a microphone (mike) for each voice and acoustic instrument. You can hold a mike but it is more convenient to put it on an adjustable stand.

Place each mike as close to its instrument as possible. A special stand called a boom can be put at any angle to bring the mike really close.

Boom stand.

Mike

Feedback

Sometimes the signal from the mike to the amp can get repeated back and forth getting louder each time, making a screaming sound called feedback. To avoid this happening, stand the mikes well away from the speakers.

PA system

To boost voices and acoustic instruments you need a PA (Public Address) system of amps and speakers. You can hire a PA from an audio equipment hire shop. It must be powerful enough to project the singer's voice to be heard above the band.

Amplifiers and speakers

Amplifiers (amps) and speakers amplify the sound of electric instruments. They come separately or as a combined unit (combo). A combo is more compact to transport.

Amps produce their sound by means of valves or transistors. Valve amps give a warm, distorted sound many rock guitarists prefer. Transistor amps give a clean, clear sound, are cheaper and reliable.

Amps are sold according to their power rating (number of watts). The more watts, the louder the sound they produce. The size of amp you need will depend on the venue, as follows:

Practice session – 15 watts
Small club   – 30 to 75 watts
Concert hall   – 100 to 200 watts

For more power, "mike" the amps to the PA as shown on the next page.

Performance set-up

Here you can see the simplest set-up for an electric and bass guitarist playing live. You can add more things such as effects boxes and a drum machine, or use more advanced equipment, as shown on the next page.

An amp increases the power of the signals from the pick-ups and mikes and converts them back into sound through the speakers. A 30 watt amp is fine for small clubs.

Mike stand placed near to singer.

Bass guitar connected to bass amp.

Bass amp.

Use a shielded, good quality lead to avoid crackle. Tuck it behind your guitar strap to stop it pulling out. Get a long lead in case you have to stand far from the equipment.

The mike converts sounds into electric signals and sends them to the PA amp. The mike is kept away from the amp to avoid feedback.

PA amp.

PA speaker.

A plug with a clamp on the lead prevents it pulling out.

Monitor speakers let you hear what you are playing.

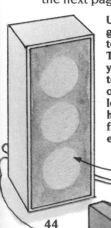

PA for large venues

If you play large venues (big halls or open-air) you need a PA mixer/amp with enough input channels to connect up the amps from all the instruments.

Mikes pick up the output (signal coming out) from each amp and feeds it into the PA mixer/amp. This is called "miking" the amp.

You will need extra powerful speakers with power amps to boost the sound level.

The input from all the instruments is balanced and amplified further, then fed out through the PA speakers.

Safety

Electrical equipment can be very dangerous. When setting up or using any equipment, make sure an expert checks extremely carefully that it has been properly wired up. A loose connection could cause a serious accident.

Advanced equipment

There are many sophisticated pieces of equipment available to aid a live performance. Here are some extra gadgets you may want to use, though they are not essential. Using this equipment would give you much better sound quality and leave you free to move about the stage and give a more lively performance. The numbered chart below shows how each piece of equipment is linked to the next.

1. A radio transmitter sends the signal from the guitar to a receiver in the amp.

2. The amp sends the signal to the effects processor.

3. The effects are controlled by a footswitch operated by the guitarist.

4. The signal returns from the effects processor to the amp.

Footswitch

Radio transmitter.

Active guitars

If you play electric guitars a lot you may be interested in buying a more sophisticated guitar. Active guitars have a built-in pre-amplifier to boost the signal from the pick-ups before it passes through leads, effects boxes and so on, where unwanted background noise may be picked up.

A digital guitar tuner allows fast, accurate tuning. You plug the guitar in, play a note and a needle indicates if the string is in tune.

A cordless mike has a radio transmitter to the PA, so you can move about on stage.

Rack-mounted effects unit.

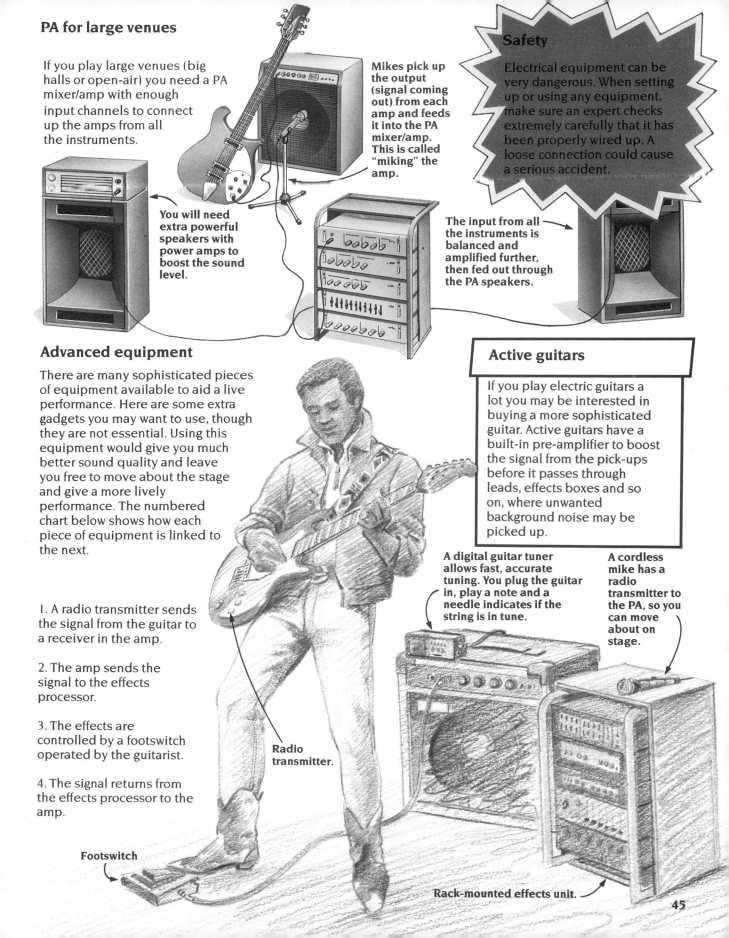

45

Strings

There are two types of guitar string – nylon and steel. Steel strings are used on electric guitars and acoustic folk guitars. Nylon strings are used on classical and flamenco guitars. If a string on your guitar breaks or stretches you will have to replace it.

Fitting strings

If you need to replace a string, you will find step-by-step guides for the different types of string on these two pages. At first it may seem rather fiddly, but you should soon be able to replace a string quite quickly with practice. These are some general tips which should help make it easier.

★ Make sure you buy the correct string for each note.

★ Replace one string at a time.

★ Remember that strings 1, 2 and 3 (the treble, or top, strings) are wound in the opposite direction to strings 4, 5 and 6 (the bass strings).

★ Attach the string at the bridge end first.

★ If you need to, trim the string with pliers at the machine head end after fitting.

★ Tune up each string as soon as you fit it.*

★ If you wipe all the sweat and dust off with a dry cloth after playing, your strings will last a lot longer.

Replacing a steel string

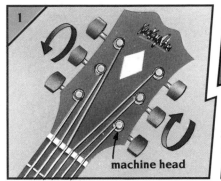

Loosen the machine head before removing a string or it could lash out and cut you. Turn the machine heads in different directions, as shown by the arrows above.

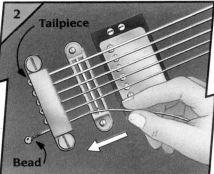

Steel strings have a bead on the end which fits into the bridge. On electric guitars, the string usually goes through a tailpiece and you must thread it out.

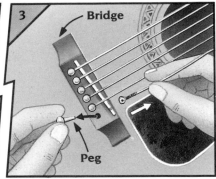

Some steel-string acoustics have small pegs to hold the beads in place. Free the string by pulling out the peg.

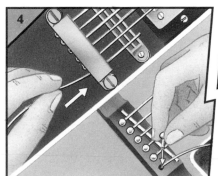

In order to fit the new string, thread the string through the bridge towards the neck, or put the bead into the hole and push in the peg.

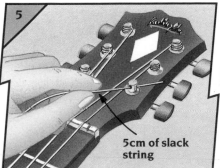

Thread the other end of the string through the machine head. Don't pull it right through, but keep 5cm (2 ins) slack to tighten the string.

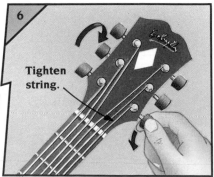

Tighten the machine head (away from the neck for bass strings and towards the neck for treble strings). Then tune* the string to the correct note.

Replacing a nylon string

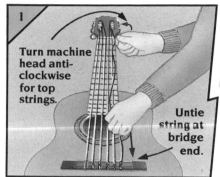

1 Turn machine head anti-clockwise for top strings. Untie string at bridge end.

To remove the old string, loosen the machine head as shown above. Pull the string out of the machine head and the bridge.

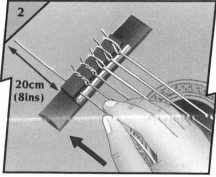

2 20cm (8ins)

Push about 20cm (8ins) of the new string through the bridge from the sound hole side. This is used for tying the string, which is described in the next step.

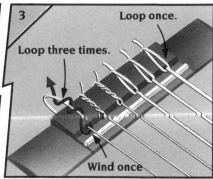

3 Loop once. Loop three times. Wind once

On strings 4, 5 and 6, wind the short end once round the rest of the string, then loop it once back round itself. On strings 1, 2 and 3, loop it back round three times.

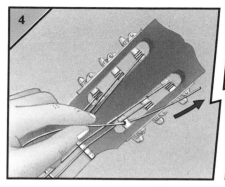

4

Pull the string tight and push the other end through the hole in the machine head. Pull it through gently to avoid twisting the string.

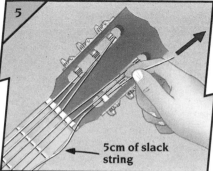

5 5cm of slack string

Don't pull the string through completely, but keep 5cm (2ins) slack so you can tighten it with the machine head.

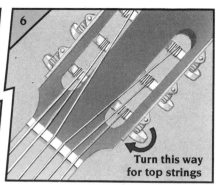

6 Turn this way for top strings

Turn the machine head (clockwise on bass strings and anti-clockwise on treble strings) to wind the slack round it and tighten the string. Then tune the string to the correct note.

Steel strings

Steel strings are made of steel, wound with nickel, silver or bronze. They are sold singly or in sets, according to the gauge (diameter) of string 1. Light-gauge strings are easiest to press down onto the frets and are the type that are used a lot in rock bands for playing loud chords. The treble strings may break more often because they are thinner than the bass strings, so buy some spares.

Strings for basses are also sold by gauge. They are thicker and more expensive than other guitar strings.

Nylon strings

Nylon strings are available in different tensions – medium, high and very high. Medium ones are easiest to press onto the frets. The crisp sound of high tension strings especially suits flamenco guitars. The bass strings are wound with metal wire and may vibrate less after a while, making them sound dull, so buy some extras. New nylon strings tend to need frequent tuning because they stretch.

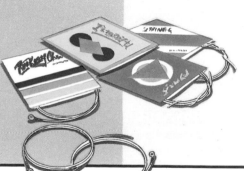

More tunes to play

On the next ten pages are a number of well-known tunes for you to play. Some are included as examples of particular styles, such as jazz or folk. Others have a new arrangement to show how various techniques you have learnt in this book can be used to change the "feel" of a piece of music. You can turn a traditional tune like Greensleeves into a heavy metal number, for example. You can try playing the tunes in different styles by experimenting yourself.

All the tunes are for two players, but you could record one part and then play the other, if you prefer. The two parts of each tune are printed on opposite pages, where appropriate, to enable two people to play together easily. Some tunes have a second part which harmonizes with the first; others have a chord accompaniment. If you are not sure of any of the chords, find them in the first half of the book, or on the chart on page 36. Play the chords in the rhythms shown.

Frankie And Johnny

A folk ballad played in a traditional way.

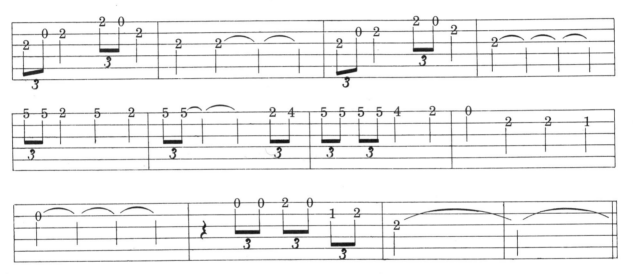

The chords and the words for the first verse of this song are on page 8.

Swing Low

This well-known gospel song is played in a slow blues style, using notes from the blues scale in C.

Part I

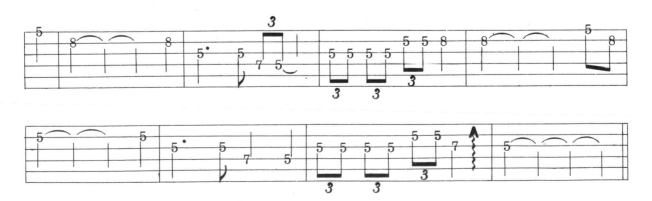

The House Of The Rising Sun

An American folk blues tune.

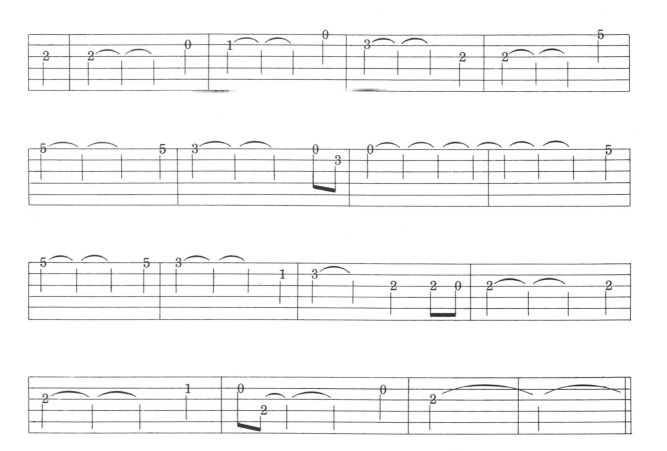

The chords and the words for the first verse of this song are on page 28.

Part II

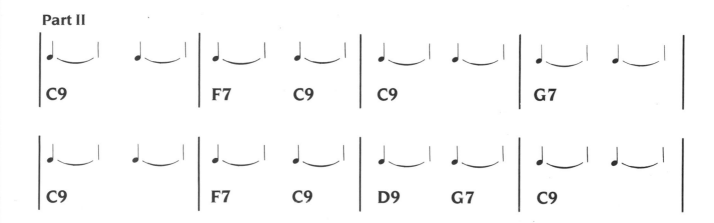

C9

F7 C9 C9 G7

C9

F7 C9 D9 G7 C9

Charlie Is My Darling

A Gaelic folk jig.

Part I

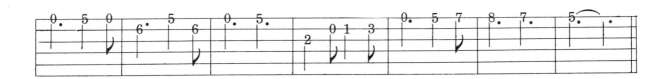

Song Of The Volga Boatmen

This traditional song has a heavy metal beat.

Part I

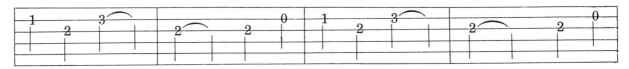

Part II

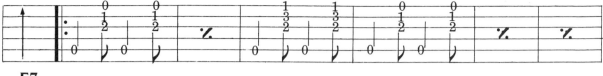

E7

Fine

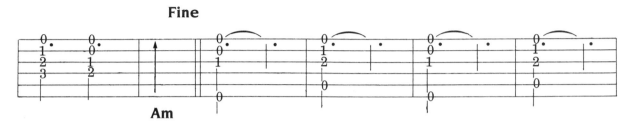

Am

D.C.al Fine

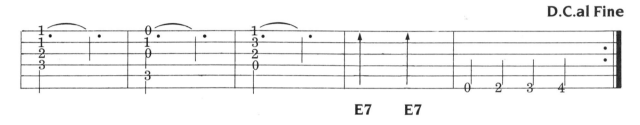

E7   E7

The bars marked * have four beats. All the other bars have just three beats.

Strum the E7 and Am chords towards you, from string 1 to string 6.

Instead of strumming the other chords, pluck the notes simultaneously.

Part II   Stress these beats.

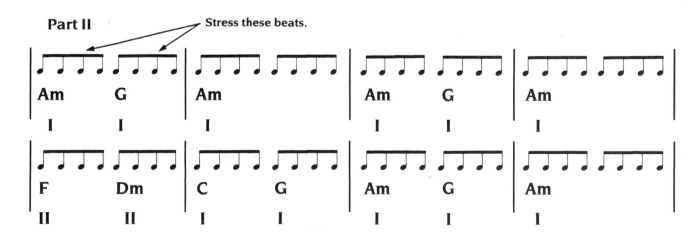

Am	G
I	I

Am
I

Am	G
I	I

Am
I

F	Dm
II	II

C	G
I	I

Am	G
I	I

Am
I

Use primary or secondary barre chords (see page 29) as marked. Play the rhythm fast, stressing the third beat each time to give this sombre, Russian folk song a raunchy rock beat.

Scarborough Fair

The arpeggios give this folk tune a classical sound.

Part I

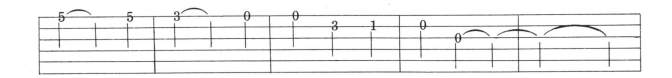

When The Saints Go Marchin' In

A fast, jazz tune with a "New Orleans" feel.

**Play this bar as an introduction.
Then start Parts I and II together.**   **Part I**

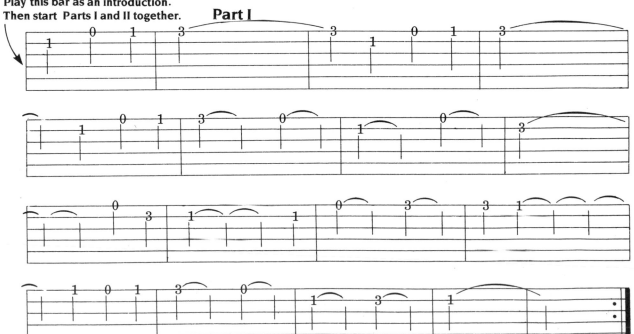

Play the introduction to Part II first.
Part I joins in after the double bar line.

Introduction **Part II**

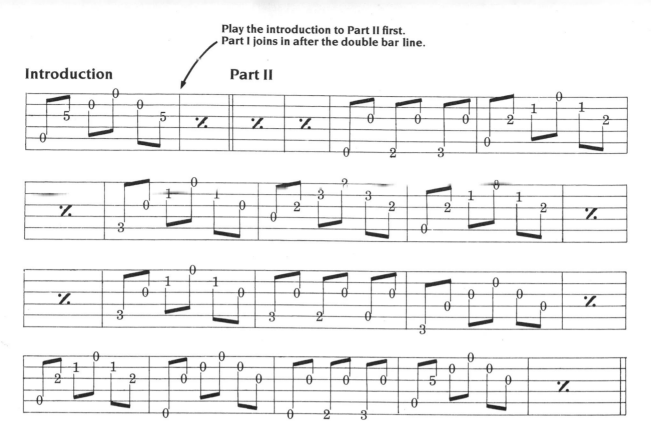

Try plucking the notes of the first bar as a chord.
Notice how the notes jar when played like this, but
sound good as an arpeggio.

Part II

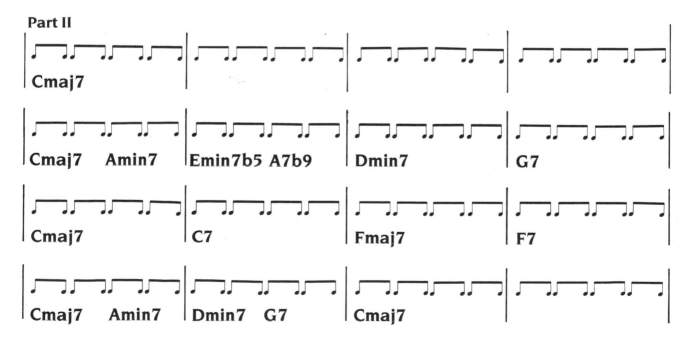

Cmaj7

Cmaj7   Amin7 | Emin7b5 A7b9 | Dmin7 | G7

Cmaj7 | C7 | Fmaj7 | F7

Cmaj7   Amin7 | Dmin7   G7 | Cmaj7

Emphasize the rhythm by damping every second quaver.

Tommy Was A Piper's Son

The finger picking style is particularly suitable for this folk tune.

Part I

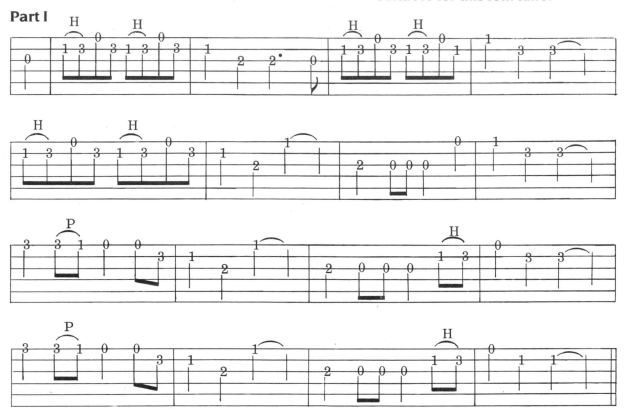

In The Hall Of The Mountain King

(from "Peer Gynt")   **Grieg**

The off-beat rhythm gives this classical tune a funky reggae feel.

Part I

Part II

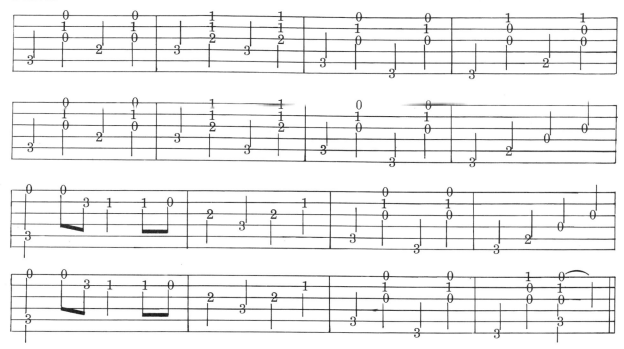

Pluck the notes of the chords together instead of strumming them.

Part II

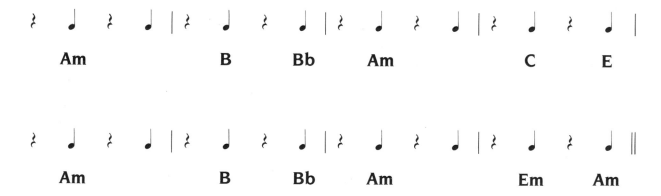

The last two lines of the tune repeat the first two, one octave higher. You can give the notes an eerie, muffled sound by pressing on the strings with your right hand, just in front of the bridge.

You could experiment with different pop beats to give other classical pieces new and unusual sounds.

Greensleeves

This version changes the feel of the tune from folk to heavy metal.

Part I

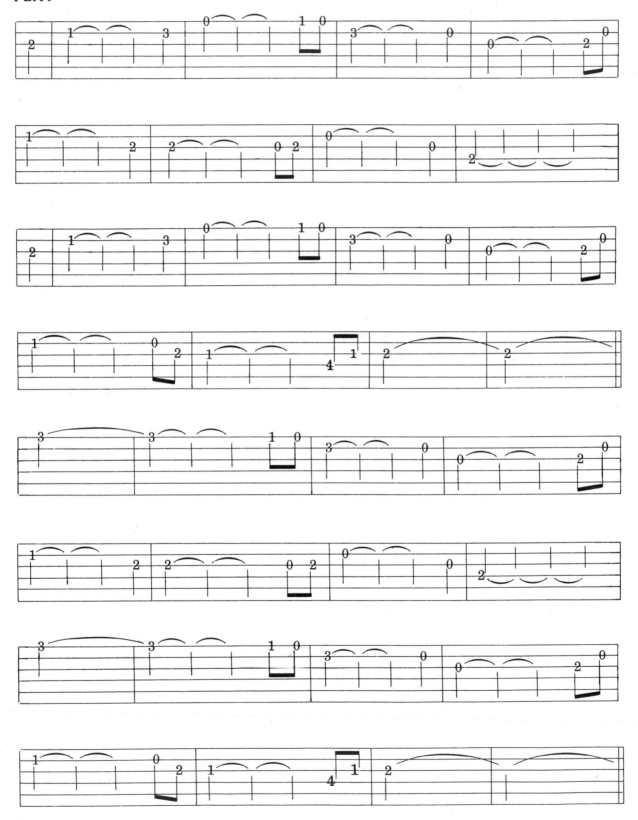

Part II

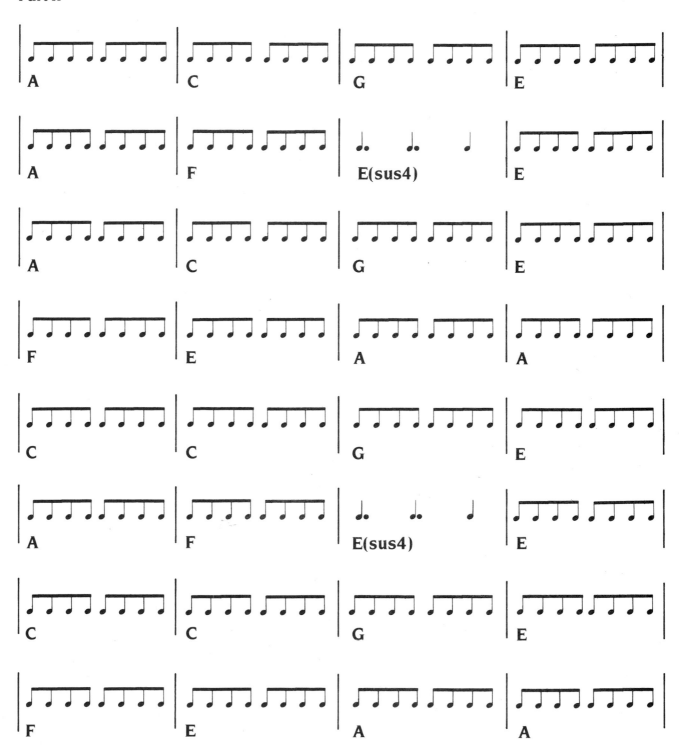

You can alter the style of a tune by using different techniques. Play a power chord backing, using the heavy rock rhythm. Play the melody loud and fast, adding trills and bending notes for effect.

Buyer's guide

Whether you opt for electric or acoustic, new or second-hand, buying your guitar should be enjoyable. Selling guitars is a sharply competitive business, so take your time to see what is available and to get an idea of prices. Try out as many guitars as you like and compare the quality. If this is your first time, take along someone who knows how to play. The real test of a guitar is how it sounds when played and how well it stays in tune. Here are some tips which may help you in your choice.

Trying out a guitar

1. Take a general look at the guitar. Is the bridge fastened on securely? Do the machine heads turn easily? Are the frets jagged? They should be polished and lying flush with the side of the fingerboard.

2. Lift the guitar up and look down the neck for any signs of warping, which would make an acoustic guitar unplayable. If the neck of an electric guitar is slightly out of line, it can be adjusted.

3. Hold the guitar as you would to play it. How does it feel? If it feels awkward or too heavy and you cannot comfortably fit your hand round the neck, try another.

4. Tune the guitar (or ask someone to do it for you). Watch closely to see if it tunes up easily or if there are any problems.

5. Pluck each string to check that each note is good. If you have time, try out each note at every fret.

6. If you have difficulty pressing the strings onto the frets, the action is too high. Any buzzing coming from the nut or the soundboard means the action is too low. If you are keen to buy that particular guitar you could have the action adjusted in a workshop, but this might be expensive.

7. For a final test, put the guitar down and look at others. Then come back to the first guitar and check to see if it is better than the others you have tried.

Tuning test

A good way to test the tuning is by playing a harmonic* at the twelfth fret of any string. The note should match exactly the fretted twelfth note. If the notes do not match on an electric guitar, the length of the strings needs adjusting. On an acoustic guitar, unmatched notes mean the neck is warped.

Tips for buying an acoustic guitar

*Look for a "solid top" label on the guitar. Those that have a soundboard made of plywood instead of solid wood are cheaper, but they produce a poorer tone.

*Most guitars have a piece of wood called a heel, which supports the back of the neck where it joins the body. Avoid guitars without a heel, as the join will be weaker and the neck liable to break off.

Tips for buying an electric guitar

*Decide if you want single coil or twin coil pickups (see page 3). Try out both styles if you are not sure.

*Operate the pickup selector switch to check that the pickups work properly.

*Try out the guitar with an amplifier. Turn all the controls up full to test for crackle.

*Compare the neck shapes and positioning of the controls on different models to see which you find most convenient to use.

*If the guitar is fitted with a tremolo arm (see page 39), make sure it presses down and returns accurately as this can affect the tuning.

*Remember that a guitar with a nice sound is more important than one that just looks good.

Buying second-hand

A good quality second-hand guitar can be much better value for money than a cheaper new one. However, only buy second-hand if you are sure of what you are looking for. You will probably not be able to exchange it and there is no guarantee that it will work. Don't be too influenced by sales talk: judge the quality of the guitar for yourself.

*Find out how to play harmonics on page 32.

Equipment guide

Guitars are available in a vast range of prices. Some people start with a less expensive model, trading it in for a better one as they advance. However, any new guitar with a price drastically lower than the average must be carefully scrutinised. Often these are badly made instruments which are not worth buying. Below are listed various popular models of different types of guitar. You will get more enjoyment from playing one that suits you and the styles you play, instead of just opting for the cheapest.

Guitar type	Recommended brands	Comments	Guitar type	Recommended brands	Comments
Nylon-string acoustic	Yamaha Alhambra	You can buy good models of these brands at reasonable prices.	Electric	Westone Epiphone Fender Yamaha Squier	Models of these brands are available in a wide price range.
Steel-string acoustic	Yamaha Fender	These can cost at least twice as much as acoustics.	Electric bass	Aria Westone	Basses are generally more expensive.
Semi-acoustic	Westone Ibanez				

Guitar extras

You may want to buy most of the items listed on the right, none of which is very expensive. If you are playing electric guitar, it is worth saving on other extras so you can buy a really good quality lead.

Plectrum	Set of strings
Capo	Lead
Guitar strap	Guitar bag

Other equipment

When choosing equipment, it is advisable to spend the most you can afford. The items on the right cost slightly more than the guitar extras above. The chart below shows examples of more expensive equipment listed roughly in order of price.

Microphone stand	Boom stand
Digital metronome	Headphones

Effects pedals	Boss	Effects pedals and mikes are not too expensive but an amp could cost as much as your guitar.	Drum machine	Boss Roland Yamaha	These items are a lot more expensive. If you play in a band, you could club together to buy them.
Microphones	Shure Audio Technica		4-Track mixer	Fostex Tascam	
Amplifier	Marshall Session Peavey		Portable studio	Fostex Amstrad Tascam	

Glossary

Action. The distance between the guitar strings and the fingerboard. Low-action guitars are easiest for a beginner to play.

Amplify. To increase the power of an electrical signal.

Arpeggio. A chord whose notes are played separately. This technique is common in classical guitar style.

Bar. A group of counts. Most of the music in this book is in bars of four counts.

Bar line. A line which divides one bar from the next. The end of a piece of music is shown by a double bar line.

Barre chord. A moveable chord shape in which your first finger presses across the strings like a bar.

Bass. A low sound. The three bass strings on a guitar make low notes. A bass guitar is tuned an octave lower than a standard guitar.

Bass/chord strum. A way of playing a chord which combines a plucked bass note and a strum.

Bass line. Notes plucked on a bass guitar or on the bass strings of a guitar.

Bass run. A folk guitar technique in which a series of notes links the bass notes of two chords.

Beat. The counts in a bar are divided into rhythmic units called beats.

Chop. A way of playing reggae chords so that they sound clipped.

Chord. A group of notes played together.

Chord sequence. A series of chords to be played one after the other.

Chord shape. The position of your left hand fingers on the neck of the guitar when playing a chord.

Clave rhythm. A West Indian rhythm traditionally played on a pair of sticks, called claves.

Click. A technique used in funky music for giving chords a muted, clicking sound.

Count. A bar is divided into equal units called counts.

Crotchet. A note of one beat.

Da capo al fine. Italian for "from the top to the end". If you see this written at the end of the music, you must repeat the first part again.

Damping. Using the left hand to muffle the vibrating strings.

Dominant 7th. The name for the third chord in a three-chord set.

Dotted note. A note followed by a dot. The dot means the note is half as long again. For example, a dotted crotchet lasts for one and a half beats.

Downstroke. A strum from the bass strings towards the top strings.

Fifth fret trick. A method of tuning the guitar, in which the strings are pressed down at the fifth fret and then plucked to see if they sound the same.

Finger picking. A style used a lot in folk music, in which each string is plucked individually.

Flat note. A note which is played one fret lower than the note of the same letter name.

Flatpicking. A plectrum technique which combines plucked strings and strumming.

Free stroke. A classical plucking technique which produces crisp, clear notes.

Fretting. Pressing down on a string behind one of the frets with a left finger.

Hammer-on. A technique that enables you to sound two notes by plucking a single string. It is used to give a distinctive folk sound to open-string chords.

Harmonics. Clear, ringing notes made by touching a string lightly at certain points while you play it.

Harmony. A combination of notes sounded together to make chords or part of a tune.

Improvise. To invent as you go along. A lot of folk music, flamenco for example, is improvised. Most improvised rock music involves making up a melody to go with an existing chord sequence.

Input. The electrical signal fed into a piece of equipment.

Key. The letter name given to a scale of notes. It is usually the same as the first note of the scale.

Key chord. The chord that begins a three-chord set and gives the set its letter name.

Key note. The bass note of a chord, which gives the chord its letter name.

Major. A major chord or scale contains eight notes separated by certain specific intervals.

Melody. A sequence of notes forming a tune.

Minor. A minor chord or scale has eight notes separated by different intervals from a major one.

Ninth chord. A moveable chord shape which includes the ninth note of a scale, much used in jazz music.

Octave. A distance of eight notes separating two notes of the same letter name.

Off-beat rhythm. A reggae rhythm, in which the second and fourth beats of a bar are stressed.

Open string. A string that is played without fretting it. On a chord diagram, this is represented by a zero.

Open-string chord. A chord that includes some open-string notes.

Output. The signal sent out by a piece of electrical equipment.

Passing notes. Plucked notes, linking the key notes of a bass line.

Picking. An alternative word for plucking (see below).

Pitch. How high or low a note sounds.

Plucking. Sounding the strings with the fingers and thumb, or with a plectrum.

Power chord. A two-string chord shape, popular in heavy metal music.

Pull-off. A technique which enables you to pluck extra notes from the neck of the guitar with your left hand.

Quaver. A note that lasts for half a beat.

Rasguado. A rapid strumming technique used in flamenco guitar.

Rest. A beat in a bar where you do not play.

Rest stroke. A classical plucking technique which produces a full, strong sound.

Rhythm. A pattern of long and short notes which makes up a melody.

Riff. A "phrase" of music, often repeated throughout a tune.

Scale. A set of notes going up or down in order. A tune is usually composed from one particular scale. On the guitar neck there are twelve frets between the first and last notes of a scale.

Semi-quaver. A note that lasts for a quarter of a beat.

Seventh chord. A moveable chord shape that includes the seventh note of a scale.

Sharp note. A note which is played one fret higher than the note of the same letter name.

Sharpened ninth chord. A variation of the ninth chord, in which the ninth note is played as a sharpened note.

Slap and pop. A way of playing bass guitar, used a lot in funky music.

Sliding chord. A chord shape, such as a ninth, that you can slide up and down the neck of the guitar to vary the pitch.

String-bending. A popular technique in blues music, in which you can give a note a moaning sound by bending the string with a left finger.

Strumming. A way of playing chords by sweeping down and up the strings with your first finger.

Sub-dominant. The name for the middle chord in a three-chord set.

Tablature. A way of writing down music for the guitar, in which the strings are represented by six horizontal lines.

Three chord trick. A set of three chords that enables you to play a vast number of tunes, especially folk and blues songs.

Tied note. A note joined to another one by a curved line. The note is played once only, and lasts for the length of both notes.

Transpose. To play a piece of music in a different key from the original one.

Treble. A high-pitched sound. The top three strings of the guitar.

Trill. A rapid alternation between a pair of notes. You play a trill by hammering-on and pulling-off notes from the same string.

Triplet. A group of three notes played in the time usually given to two.

Tune up. To adjust the pitch of the strings to make the correct sounds.

Upstroke. An upwards strum from the top strings to the bass strings.

Vibrato. A vibrating note made by vibrating a string with a left finger.

Discography

Below are listed the different styles of music covered in this book with suggested guitarists and bands to listen to. Each album listed is a particularly good example of a guitarist's work, but if you cannot find the album mentioned, try listening to another by the same artist.

Traditional blues

Eric Clapton	E.C. Was Here
B.B. King	Live At The Regal
Albert King	
Muddy Waters	
Johnny Winter	Nothin' But The Blues

Rock 'n' roll

Allman Brothers Band	At Fillmore East
Chuck Berry	
Cream	Best Of Cream
Ten Years After	Woodstock

Folk

Bob Dylan	Nashville Skyline
Fairport Convention	Unhalfbricking
Pentangle	Pentangling
Paul Simon	Sounds Of Silence

Country

Chet Atkins	
Grateful Dead	Workingman's Dead
Albert Lee	

Heavy Metal

Def Leppard	Hysteria
Jimi Hendrix and The Experience	Are You Experienced
Iron Maiden	Powerslave
Led Zeppelin	Led Zeppelin
Motorhead	Ace of Spades

Reggae

Aswad	Rebel Souls
Black Uhuru	Brutal
Bob Marley and The Wailers	Natty Dread
The Police	The Police

Flamenco

Paco de Lucia	The Fabulous Guitar Of Paco de Lucia
Paco Pena	The Art Of The Flamenco Guitar

Jazz/funk

Jeff Beck	Wired
Chick Corea	Return To Forever
Herbie Hancock	Headhunters

Soul/funk

James Brown	
Sly and the Family Stone	Greatest Hits
Tina Turner	Private Dancer

Classical

Julian Bream	
The Romeros	
Andres Segovia	
John Williams	
Julian Bream and John Williams	Together

Traditional jazz

Charlie Christian	
Wes Montgomery	
Django Reinhardt	

Jazz rock

George Benson	Live In Concert
Larry Coryell	Eleventh House At Montreaux
Al Dimeola	Elegant Gypsy
Allan Holdsworth	U.K.
John Mahavishnu McLaughlin	Birds Of Fire

Rhythm

Dire Straits	Dire Straits
The Pretenders	The Pretenders

Electric bass

Stanley Clarke	Stanley Clarke

Index

First published in 1988 by Usborne Publishing Ltd, 20, Garrick Street, London WC2E 9BJ, England.

Copyright © Usborne Publishing Ltd. 1988
The name Usborne and the device 🎈 are Trade Marks of Usborne Publishing Ltd.

Printed in Great Britain.

Photographs courtesy of David Redfern Photography. Photograph of Andres Segovia courtesy of Clive Barda Photography – London.